Appearances Speak Louder Than Words

by
Teri Twitty-Villani

Voyager Press
Portland, Oregon

If you think you are beaten , you are;
If you think you dare not, you don't.
If you'd like to win, but think you can't,
It's almost a cinch you won't.
If you think you'll lose, you're lost,
For out in the world we find
Success begins with a fellow's will,
It's all in the state of mind.

If you think you're out classed, you are;
You've got to think high to rise.
You've got to be sure of yourself before
You can ever win a prize.
Life's battles don't always go
To the stronger or faster man;
But soon or late the man who wins
Is the one who thinks he can.

Walter D. Wintle

Acknowledgments

I always thought "thank yous" in books were boring and silly but now that I have been through the process of writing this one I have some people I can't thank enough.

I would like to thank:

All of my clients and customers for letting me use their stories and opinions. No one has better women clients. I can honestly say that I am a better person for having worked with the variety of personalities and professions that they represent.

Alex, no little sister could be more loving, supportive and efficient at the same time.

Jody for making me look in the mirror when times got stressed and for seeing the good and the purpose.

Margaret for being so sure of me and showing it freely, and for her total acceptance and nonjudgmental love and caring.

Dorothy for a friendship that gives me escape, and an opinion that is objective and on target with my purposes.

Mom because you live a positive life and raised us to see the good in others and in life. A gift I now realize few people are blessed with.

Gramma because of the example of spirit and confidence she has shown all my life.

Curry who has fixed my computer, my car, my dinner, my schedule and me when I most needed it. And for always wanting what's best for me, even when I don't. For being there through the drudgery and still smiling.

Introduction

This book is written to help you on your road to happiness and success.

Life is a journey. We all have different destinations. You may map out your trip but you can't see the potholes, bridges out or detours until you get to them. The vehicle you choose on any journey makes the difference as to how much you enjoy the ride, and whether or not you will arrive at where you want to go.

Nonverbal communication and dress are a reliable and effective vehicle for making your journey through life more successful and enjoyable. Through improved nonverbal communication you can develop an image that projects your positive personality traits. As a result you will be understood better. This will help to prevent conflict (potholes), stress (bridges out), and misunderstandings (detours).

When you feel understood you develop better relationships and healthy self esteem. By learning improved nonverbal communication and dress you will be acting to smooth some of the bumps and bruises you'll encounter on the road to success.

Table of Contents:

List Of Illustrations

Cross-Overs

1

"Whosoever hath a good presence and a good style, carries continual letters of recommendation."
Isabella of Spain

There is almost nothing in this world you can't do or be if you have a positive attitude and self esteem. This is a statement with which few people would argue, and yet with all the good books, persuasive teachers and inspirational video and audio tapes available on how to strengthen self esteem and create positive attitude both goals seem to be illusive. Only about two percent of the people who read the books, listen to the tapes and go to seminars actually take action on what they learn. One of the main reasons for this is that what people hear does not coincide with what they see. You may say you are a winner, but if you don't look like one you won't believe it.

Can you really boost your self esteem simply by improving your appearance? Yes! Through nonverbal communication you can present yourself as a winner if you know how. When you look and act like a winner, you begin to think like one. The fact is, you can choose to talk or not, but you can't be silent in nonverbal communication even if you are naked and bald. Since you are going to be *saying* something about yourself think how helpful it would be for you to know what it is you're saying, and if it is positive, think how powerful for your self esteem that would be.

We are not born with the ability to use words, but we are born with the ability to communicate. An infant can express hunger without words, or show that it doesn't feel well. But communication isn't just for physical survival. People have emotional and intellectual needs that are just as important. Among these is the need to be understood, to be appreciated, and to be loved. None of these basic human needs can be met without communication, and all of these can be communicated without the use of words. In fact, many times words only interfere with the message and make it more difficult to be understood.

Even though 75 to 90 percent of effective communication is nonverbal our American education system teaches us virtually nothing about it. We advance our learning through experience, but even this is difficult because we rarely get feedback on how we are doing. With so little time spent on this important and valuable skill, it is no wonder we have trouble understanding and relating to each other.

It is the instinct to communicate that makes it impossible to be silent even when you don't speak. You can't ignore grimaces of pain even if a person is saying she feels fine. You can't ignore a sorrowful tone of voice even when a person says she is happy. You can't ignore a person's look of disarray even if she professes to be organized. If you met a dirty, ragged, barefoot man and he told you he was a millionaire would you believe him? If you met a thirty-year-old woman with a lot of makeup, skin tight clothes, and a wiggle that wouldn't quit would you see her as a naive, innocent person? If you were introduced to a woman who looked down at her shoes all the time, wore no make up, slumped her shoulders and barely talked above a whisper would you believe that she was a powerful corporate executive?

Most of us can recognize how often we use nonverbal clues to make decisions about others and what they are saying. Yet we tend to deny the importance of what we are saying about ourselves—both to our reflection in the mirror and to others. If your reflection in the mirror does not support your positive attributes, then it undermines your belief in yourself and hinders the work you are doing to improve yourself or your life. I often hear the comment, "People should just take me for who I am." That's fine; but should others believe what you *say* or what they *see*? Like you, they will believe their eyes more than their ears. With the positive use of nonverbal communication hearing and seeing can be consistent.

Let's say you are in a job interview and the main traits the manager is looking for in the person he is about to hire are organizational skills and reliability. You are aware of this and know you would be an excellent candidate for the position. Instead of portraying the qualities the manager is seeking you walk in and say, *"Hi, I am a blast at a party and I love going shopping."* Seems ridiculous doesn't it? But women do it all the time with their nonverbal communication and then wonder why they are misunderstood or unappreciated. In personal relationships they often say nonverbally, *"I have a great body and I want you to desire it,"* when all along it's their gentle and loving side they want the man to see. The sad part is that we blame the other person for not seeing us for "who we are." That is as silly as telling someone you're an accountant and labeling him insensitive because he doesn't realize you're really an electrician.

Through positive nonverbal communication you can make educated and conscious decisions about how others see you. No longer will you have to leave those decisions up to luck or chance. Through this process you will become more willing to take responsibility for how you are perceived and you will not be able to place the credit or blame on someone else. Actually, the process is a never ending cycle: If you want to become a more organized person, first you have to present yourself as organized. Then you begin to see yourself as organized, you act more organized, others treat you as organized, and finally, you believe it. Now you are organized.

I feel a little silly admitting that it took me 13 years as a student and teacher in self improvement to discover that the biggest support for having good self esteem and a winning attitude was in my own mirror. It's so simple and that is why it's so effective. You believe what you see. Project yourself as a winner and you will believe it. No matter how many classes you take, books you read or tapes you listen to on how to best love yourself or develop good relationships, it won't work if nonverbally you are saying something else.

Remember 75 to 90 percent of what you believe about yourself and what others believe about you comes from seeing it, not hearing it.

NONVERBAL

The One Truly Great Art Of Communication.

It is appearance that best reflects your self respect and individuality. Your image communicates simply and effectively once you learn the language. Whether reliable, practical and honest or wild, flamboyant and sexy, you are the only you in all the world. There has never been another you in all of history and there never will be again. You will always be the very best at being you and second best at being anyone else. Why settle for second best when being number one is more fun, more satisfying and more respected.

> *You will always be the very best at being you and second best at being anyone else.*

Truly dressing for success is learning to: Express the positives in who you are or strive to be; reflect self confidence, self respect and self-love; and doing it all within the guidelines of the world in which you live or choose to live.

But getting "dressed" is more than the clothes you wear or how you do your hair. It is also:

°°°A Smile
°°°Eye Contact

°°°Tone Of Voice
°°°Touch
°°°Active Listening
°°°Facial Expressions
°°°Body Language
°°°Health, Fitness and Hygiene

Neglecting any of these will cause misconceptions and misunderstandings about who you are and how you wish to be treated. On its own each quality is worth a thousand words. We simply need to understand the value of each quality and how to use it to best advantage.

The Magic Of A Smile

An inexpensive way to improve your looks.

You know how much a smile means to you when you see it on someone else. Do you realize the wonder it holds when you wear it yourself? Smile at yourself in the mirror tomorrow morning. In fact make it a habit every time you see your own reflection. Give yourself a warm and pleasing smile. It takes no time and no money and it will make all the difference in your day.

When you buy groceries and you walk up to the counter the clerk greets you with a big, warm, welcoming smile. The next day you go to the store and a different clerk checks you through. He nods and says "Hello"...no smile. Which clerk do you like better? The one who smiled, of course; we all do. A smile communicates several things which our society holds in high regard.

> *A smile is a gift to another person.*
> *If you smile in the mirror it is a gift to yourself.*

When you smile you are saying to the other person that you are making an effort for a moment to make her feel a little better or more at ease. When you smile you are saying, "I wish you well and no harm." When you smile you exude confidence and a good attitude. If you want to be seen as some one who cares and can be trusted you need to learn to put a smile on your face.

7

A lot of my clients have said to me, "It's fake if you smile when you don't feel like it. I can't do that." Oh, no it isn't and yes you can. There is nothing fake about greeting someone with a smile even if you just found out that you're getting audited. A smile does not say, "I am a person with no problems and everything is perfect."

A smile is a gift to another person. If you smile in the mirror it is a gift to yourself. The giving of a gift is not reserved for the times in our lives when everything is going well.

Two years ago a very shy, meek, intelligent, whisper of a woman came to me for assistance. I was impressed that Kim had gathered up the courage to ask for help. The first thing I did with her was to take her to the grocery store down the road. Every aisle we went through I would greet people and say "Hi." After about five minutes I asked if she noticed anything. She said that obviously I was greeting people but that most people were not very friendly. She told me that she had no desire to set herself up for this kind of rejection. I acknowledged her concern and then said let's give it five more minutes.

As I walked around the store I greeted people this time with a warm smile along with the "Hi." Every person returned the smile. Every person returned the greeting. Several people said something more to us ranging from, "Isn't it a nice day?" to "Don't you love the produce here?" After about three minutes Kim said how different these people were from the others we had met. She asked me if I knew why and of course being the cooperative person that I am, I told her. As she talked to me Kim was smiling.

Kim had come to me planning to leave as a new person. She was startled when I told her that we were finished for the day. Then I gave her an assignment and made her next appointment with me.

Kim's assignment was to greet every person with a smile, stranger or not, and to write down her comments on what she observed. A week later Kim greeted me with a beautiful smile, a hug and left me with this note:

"I don't know how to say thank you because I don't know if I understand what has happened this past week. After I left you I was less than excited about doing the assignment, but I did. The following morning at work I began greeting people with a smile and I kept it up as much as possible the entire week. In fact, my jaw got tired.

"In eight years with my company I have never been asked out to lunch by my associates; I have now been invited three times. I also have made a new friend in my neighborhood. What really surprised me was that a woman at work, who I always thought disliked me, is now greeting me every morning."

For a long time this wonderfully warm, kind, thoughtful person had been so caught up in her own feelings of inadequacy that she didn't smile. When you make the choice not to smile you are being self involved and often self pitying. Is that the way you wish to be seen?

It is not only the meek and those who lack confidence who don't smile. A smile is also the main force that keeps us from being cranks, nags, and downers. It is like a wonderful perfume which you can't pour on others without getting a little on yourself.

A Smile is:

Whispering laughter.

The best umbrella in the world on a rainy day, even in Oregon.

An instant vacation.

<u>Exercise # 1</u>:

When you look into a mirror, before you do anything else smile at yourself. Make it a habit.

<u>Exercise # 2</u>:

Go into a public place and for the first five minutes walk by people and greet them without a smile. For the next five minutes greet everyone with a warm smile. Notice the difference in your attitude and that of others. This makes a fun and inexpensive date.

Eye Contact

The pulse of the soul; as physicians judge the heart
by the pulse, so we by the eye.
                                        Thomas Adams

"I'll believe what you say if you look me in the eye." This statement reflects the common belief that the eyes speak the truth. It is not natural to lie with your eyes and to do it takes a lot of work. So if you want someone to trust you, look into his eyes. This is, bar none, the most important expression of honesty.

Eye contact also is one of the best ways to get someone's attention. When the speaker at a seminar looks you right in the eye you pay more attention. When your kids aren't taking you seriously, you stop everything you are doing and establish eye contact. Across a crowded room you can tell your partner you are ready to leave with just your eyes.

When you look someone in the eyes you are telling him more about the way you think or feel than any words ever could. If you are tired your eyes say so. If you are happy, angry, sad, dreamy, anxious, lonely, or even if you are ill, the eyes reflect it. So the next time you can't find the right words to express an emotion, start by looking the person in the eye.

When you neglect to look someone in the eye it is interpreted as, "What you are saying is not as important as what I am doing or thinking," or "I don't really believe what I'm telling you." It may even be translated as "I am no good and I am someone to feel sorry for." If you want good relationships you must learn to look people in the eye.

---

*When you look someone in the eyes
you are telling him more about the way you think
or feel than any words ever could.*

I have a customer who has been blind since birth. She is a doctor of psychology and has a company that helps handicapped graduate students obtain grants and corporate sponsorships. Her pet peeve is other people who express pity and a lack of professionalism when they discover she is blind. Caroline's reason for coming to see me was to learn how to dress and express herself in a more serious and professional manner.

With an enthusiastic and feisty personality like Caroline's, I was hesitant to teach her to present herself as too serious. Although she had been hindered by not being seen as a professional, I was confident that her spirit was the main reason for her success. Presenting herself as stiff and controlled was not the answer. Her style would actually become more comfortable and lively than it had been before. In order to develop the image of a more competent and successful woman, she needed to learn to look people in the eye even though she was blind.

By locating the eyes of people speaking to her from the sound of their voices Caroline was able to look at them directly and confidently. They began to listen and pay attention to what she said. Last year I heard this amazing woman speak in front of graduating high school seniors. She talked about making choices and taking responsibility for your life. She was so good at eye contact and looking through the audience that she had to tell the listeners at the end of her speech that she was blind. What an impact! The audience was stunned and gave her a standing ovation.

When I called and asked Caroline if I could use her story, she said "YES," as long as I included this observation: "When you look someone in the eye they silently applaud you because of your honesty and courage. When you avoid the eyes all the applause is out of pity or a sense of responsibility. With total lack of vision I have experienced the power of the eyes. Your eyes are not just to see color or light, they are also your messengers of integrity and truth."

The Eyes are:

> *The light of the body.*
>> *Bible: Matthew, VI,22.*
>
> *The windows of the soul.*
>> *Guillaume Du Bartas*
>
> *The peephole of the consciousness.*
>> *Elbert Hubbard*
>
> *That which tells what the heart means.*
>> *Judah Lazerov*

Exercise #1:

Stand in front of a mirror and look directly into your own eyes. For 5 minutes say nothing but good things about yourself. You'll begin to truly believe those things and you will increase your self esteem.

<u>Exercise #2</u>:

Stare into the eyes of the person you love for 30 seconds and say nothing. Then try it for 60 seconds the next time. Notice the feelings that arise. Are you uncomfortable? Do you giggle from embarrassment? Keep working at it. It breaks down all kinds of emotional barriers.

<u>Exercise #3</u>:

If there is a person at work or in your personal life who you feel doesn't understand you, work diligently to make eye contact with him whenever you have a conversation.

Tone Of Voice

The actual face behind the mask of words.

Isn't it amazing how many different meanings the word "fine" has when you are asked, "How are you?" A common meaning for the word fine in retail is: "I don't want anybody selling me anything so keep your distance." When your spouse uses this word he may mean: "Things would be better if I hadn't had to come home to a dirty kitchen." The girl at the office might mean, "I feel blue and I want you to know it. Please feel sorry for me."

There really is no end to what some words can actually mean. The meaning is derived from the way a person says it. The clue is in the tone of voice.

I don't know about you but when I was growing up one of my mother's most common reprimands was, "Don't use that tone of voice with me, young lady." I would like to believe that when I matured beyond being a "young lady" my ability to use tone of voice naturally matured. It didn't; it took a lot of work. It takes work for all of us.

Your tone of voice will cause you more arguments, disagreements and misunderstandings than your spoken words ever will. It will also bring you more peace, harmony and understanding than words do. When your tone is in conflict with your words it may be because you are thinking about something entirely different or it may be that you think you are hiding how you really feel. Regardless of the reasons, you need to be conscious of your tone of voice if you want people to believe your words.

There is one tone of voice that all winners have.

15

ENTHUSIASM! Without it sincerity and truth don't stand a chance of being victorious. Enthusiasm is contagious and it makes life much more pleasant. When you speak with enthusiasm you are sending nothing but positive messages. You are putting conviction into your words. We like people who get to the issue and get things done—enthusiasm says just that.

> *There is one tone of voice that all winners have.*
> *ENTHUSIASM!*
> *Without it sincerity and truth*
> *don't stand a chance of being victorious.*

Do you remember your teachers who were enthusiastic about what they taught? Do you remember the ones who weren't?

The only people who can be enthusiastically <u>negative</u> are comedians who produce one of the most positive wonders of the world...laughter.

At 47, Lisbeth, through diligence and hard work, had become executive secretary for a CEO in an international company. When we met four years ago she was quite controlled, organized, responsible and bored. She was respected in her job and had the authority to mold the kind of staff she wanted. Her boredom and unhappiness had nothing to do with her duties. She felt that her job advancement had distanced her from others with whom she had shared activities in the past, such as the company softball team. Now, the only events in which she was included were the more formal evening affairs.

I asked her, "Do you like your job?"

She said, "Yes, it's a good position."

With enthusiasm in my voice, a big smile, and leaning forward in my chair I asked, "Lisbeth do you like your job? Tell me how much with your voice. Is it exciting to have worked up to such a wonderful position? Tell me with your voice. Do you like your boss? Tell me with the tone of your voice."

I was certain that her sensitivity to changes in the way other employees treated her was a result of her own attitude. Her voice lacked enthusiasm so people saw her as much more serious and controlled than she actually was.

The following week I asked Lisbeth to practice Exercise #1 that appears in this section of the book. I also asked her to put enthusiasm into her voice in all business conversations. These are excerpts from her journal which she shared with me:

Week 1: "I don't think anyone is treating me differently, but I certainly have had a more productive and enjoyable week."

Week 2: "They do still have a softball team and I will be playing as a substitute next Tuesday."

Week 3: "I received verbal praise from two superiors this week and the sales manager asked me if I'd had a face lift (jokingly) and said I looked ten years younger."

By changing the tone of her voice to be more positive, Lisbeth had created a positive chain reaction.

One year later when she stopped by she left this note:

Dear Teri:

I'm having a blast and in fact have incorporated your tone of voice and appearance exercises into all training for our employees in customer service, clerical, management and sales.

I know I fought you tooth and nail on the idea that my environment was what I had made it. Becoming conscious of my voice tone has helped my happiness and the entire environment at work. We have fewer miscommunications than ever before. The team work we have developed was an unexpected asset.

By the way, I have a new man in my life and he is a real go-getter. With sincerity and enthusiasm I say thank you for being the catalyst to my growth.

Take care,

    Lisbeth

Learn to put enthusiasm in your voice and you will make your life a lot easier, more pleasant and more fun.

The Voice is:

> *A second face.*
>
>   *Gerard Bauer*
>
> *An index of character.*
>
> *A direct path to the heart.*
>
> *Nothing great was ever achieved without enthusiasm.*
>
>   *Emerson*
>
> *Every great and commanding moment in the annals of the world is the triumph of some enthusiasm.*
>
>   *Emerson*

Exercise #1:

> You must be aware of and exert control over voice tone. Like any other part of the body, if it is not used, it can get rusty. It needs exercise to get into winning shape. Imagine

that you have just been asked, "How are you today?" Think about it a minute, then answering with just the word "Fine," express the following:

°°°Enthusiasm
°°°Impatience
°°°Joy
°°°Boredom
°°°Sadness
°°°Anger
°°°Sincerity
°°°Warmth
°°°Sexiness
°°°Shyness
°°°Doubt
°°°Dreamy
°°°Peace
°°°Surprise.

You can add to the list of emotions and change words as well.

Word suggestions:

Yes...No...Now...Great...Maybe... Nothing...When...What...

Options:

Tape record yourself.
Do it with others.
Play it as a game in the car.
Use it in staff meetings to develop positive attitude and improve communication.

<u>Exercise #2</u>:

Write as many emotions or expressions as you can think of on small slips of paper and put them into a container. Use those in Exercise # 1 to get started. Then put all kinds of crazy words into a separate container. Have each person draw out one slip from each container. The object is for each person to portray the emotion designated on the slip using the word given. Teammates have to guess what emotion the player is trying to convey. You can put a time limit on the game or you can limit the number of responses each player is allowed.

Touch

*Devils can be driven out of the heart by the touch
of a hand on a hand...*
Tennessee Williams

The touch of the hand can bring calm to the harried, joy to the sad, warmth to the lonely, contentment to the angry or it can bring fury, pain, and discomfort. When you touch another human being you break the invisible line of defense. When you learn to use touching as a positive tool you will be able to change almost any negative situation into a positive one—a moment to remember.

When you are in disagreement with someone, the situation can get pretty heated. The more important that person is to you the greater the possibility for strong emotions. Picture yourself in an argument with someone precious to you. You are 15 minutes late and the person jumps on you the minute you arrive. Just say the words, "I'm sorry." Now reach across the table, softly touch your friend's hand, look into his eyes and say, "I'm sorry." With that approach you have broken down some of his defenses. He believes you. You have shown sincere caring.

You still may think that he overreacted and that in fact you arrived on time. You can choose to be right and argue about it, or choose to have a nice evening. Most people don't care as much about being right as they do about being understood. By offering understanding you have diffused his anger.

Last year while I was on a business trip, a flight I was scheduled to take was canceled. I was in Los Angeles and needed to be in Chicago by eight o'clock the next morning. More than 400 people would be waiting there for me to speak to them. I was sent to another airline. When I arrived the ticket agent seemed harried. Everything about him was (nonverbally) screaming. I told him my tale of woe. I wanted him to do everything he could to get me a flight. I also wanted to be sure that *he* understood *my* dilemma.

He looked at me and said, "I'm sorry but we have absolutely nothing until tomorrow morning and I have ten ahead of you who want the same thing."

I was frustrated to say the least. I knew that the way I approached him would determine whether or not I got what I wanted. I said, "You must be tired of all the people getting upset with you because they can't get the flight they want. Not one of your better days I imagine." Then I reached across the counter, lightly patted his hand and said, "I was watching you when I was in line and you are really doing a great job maintaining a good attitude. I know this is not your fault and I would appreciate anything that you could do for me." I made sure he knew *I* understood *his* dilemma.

He relaxed visibly, smiled, touched my arm and said, "Thank you, let me see what I can do." Only fifteen minutes later, I was on my way to Chicago.

He had built up such a wall of defense to guard himself against the offensive behavior of unhappy passengers. No one had taken the time to understand what it was like to be on his side of the problem. Giving him a light touch on the arm was a quick and sincere way to get on his side of the wall. I had made a friend. Don't we all do a little extra for the people we like—the people who touch us with a smile, a reassuring hand?

The Handshake

There are several types of touches that are accepted and powerful in our culture. One very important touch to master is the handshake. It is a custom in our society. The manner of a handshake helps to convey social and business savvy. A good handshake communicates confidence, friendliness, enthusiasm, integrity and much more.

With just the shake of a hand you can make or break existing and potential business relationships. A good handshake can really set a woman apart. Women typically don't execute a good, firm handshake, but when one does it impresses the recipient—especially men.

With just the shake of a hand you can make or break existing and potential business relationships.

I have a client who got a second job interview because she so impressed her potential boss with her handshake. This set her apart from the other applicants. Of course, it took more than the handshake to qualify her for the position, but without it her chances would have been much slimmer.

The person who offers her hand first communicates confidence and integrity.

When you shake hands put the "V" of your thumb

and index finger into the "V" of the other person's hand and return equal pressure. If you offer your hand before the other person, be sure the palm is facing slightly up. This gesture communicates openness and friendliness. The person who offers her hand first communicates confidence and integrity. Holding on to a person's hand while she expresses a quick greeting or thought communicates, "You have my undivided attention."

If you wish to express a little affection, simply reach out with your other hand and touch the hand or arm that you are shaking. If you wish to communicate, "It's good to see you," reach out with your hand and pat the back of the person's hand you are greeting.

You want to avoid pumping a person's hand or arm. Many people see this as presumptuous. Instead, show enthusiasm by getting your hand out there, smiling and looking into the person's eyes.

The "dainty" hand shake is a communication of submissiveness and weakness. There was a time when women didn't shake hands; they merely offered their hand to a gentleman; it was a submissive act. Our roles have certainly changed, and our handshake should reflect that change.

Then there is the "limp rag" shake. This actually disgusts most people. They view it as a sign of femininity in a man and a lack of intelligence in a woman. In either gender it is viewed as a weakness.

Many women today are still shy about shaking hands. Teachers, for example, tell me that they don't see any reason for shaking hands in their profession. No matter where you are or what you are doing it can't hurt to communicate all the positive things a good handshake offers. Words just don't do it as well.

When I go to social and professional affairs I often

see women who *appear* together and confident. They lose the good impression they could make because they have a poor handshake. Ask a few men you respect—other than your spouse—if they believe you have a good handshake. If they hesitate, be sure to reassure them that you really want to know. Then actually practice shaking hands. Please don't be embarrassed; most men start shaking hands as toddlers. Our culture leaves it up to women to stumble onto an appropriate handshake on their own.

The Hug

Another acceptable and highly appreciated touch is the hug. A bad day is made better with a hug. A hug can be an expression of caring, warmth, friendship, tenderness, kindness, concern, sharing, joy, relief, understanding, enthusiasm and security. It can be given as a gift to loved ones, recent acquaintances and even female business associates.

When it feels right to hug someone, don't hesitate. Few things can create a bond between people like a hug. To insure appropriate behavior at work, a hug should be given, not taken. In other words, if you just had a heated discussion with a co-worker which you now feel is resolved and you want to let her know there are no hard feelings a hug can do it. If on the other hand you want to be hugged because *you* feel badly and need to be reassured, opt for the handshake. A hug in this situation can be uncomfortable.

Unfortunately, giving a hug to a man in the work place may be misconstrued. The line is a dangerous one to cross. Be careful. You can communicate your caring attitude by other touches. A pat on the back, a touch on the arm, a gentle punch in the shoulder all communicate positive things about you and how you feel about the recipient of your attention. If you are not the "touching kind" that's fine, but be aware touching makes you more approachable and closes the distance between you and others.

Exercise #1:

> The next time you have something to say to a loved one which you think may result in a defensive or negative response, sit next to that person and hold his hand while you speak. If it is not a close relationship and doesn't warrant hand-holding, sit next to him and periodically touch his arm, shoulder, or hand.
>
> If it is a business relationship sit next to the person rather than across a desk and be sure to end the conversation with a handshake.

Exercise #2:

> Give out three hugs a day. Make note of how much happier your days turn out to be.

Active Listening

It is the easiest way to persuade others.

Rarely if ever taught in our society, listening is one of the most respected and admired of all the communication skills. It communicates intelligence, thoughtfulness and graciousness more powerfully than anything else. If you want to have successful relationships at work or at home you must learn to actively listen. There is no substitute.

Listening is the silent voice of understanding. Being understood is the most sought after basic human need of our time. In order to understand someone else you must listen. This means using your ears to hear, your heart and mind to listen. Lack of understanding causes divorce, bankruptcy, desolation and even war. Once you work on your listening skills you will also experience the side benefit of feeling more understood yourself.

> *Listening is the silent voice of understanding.*

Understanding and agreeing are not the same thing. You can understand why a person fed his family by stealing but you may not agree with the method.

"A man convinced against his will is of the same opinion still." -Anonymous. How many pro-life advocates do you think have had their minds changed by pro-choice supporters? What would happen to this issue if the opponents sat down, listened and simply tried to

understand the other side? I'm not talking agreement—I don't believe with such an emotional issue that it is possible. I mean simply, understanding. If you try to resolve an issue without understanding, the fight will continue forever or remain a sore spot. Whenever a person stops trying to be right and starts trying to understand, conflict dissolves.

> *Understanding and agreeing are not the same thing.*

Although eye contact can be the best way to communicate the fact that you are indeed listening, active listening requires much more. You need to give your full attention to the person talking to you. Stop what you're doing and look at the person talking. We are so busy today that we don't take time to listen. In fact you waste time by not listening because it creates misconceptions and misunderstandings which eat up energy and time.

> *Whenever a person stops trying to be right*
> *and starts trying to understand, conflict dissolves.*

It's a fallacy to believe that while your boss is telling you about a meeting that went badly you can get up, get a cup of coffee and still be listening attentively. Have you heard yourself saying, "I'm still listening, go ahead." Of course you have. You might have been using your ears, but you were not listening.

The person who is talking resents your lack of attention when you walk away from him. He may cut what he was going to say short, or stop completely because he feels you don't value his words. He will certainly lose respect for you.

While the other person is talking most people are waiting for their chance to talk. This means they are not listening and it shows up in all kinds of ways, such as interrupting. When you are talking to an adult and a child comes in and interrupts your conversation what do you usually say? Why is it any different for you as an adult? Aren't we supposed to have better manners than a child? I recently had a good friend tell me I had interrupted him twice in one evening. It is so embarrassing to be so blatantly human. I made it a priority to work on it. I have always known it to be rude, but I had slipped into a bad habit.

Another important active listening skill is acknowledgment. This can be done with a nod of the head or eye contact. Even a change of facial expression or a certain touch can convey the fact that you are listening. When it comes to developing listening skills we need to consciously work on them and be consistent about using them. It takes constant work to be a good listener; it is not a born talent. Have you ever heard anyone say, "She is too good a listener?" When I teach a class on communication women always complain that their men don't ever talk to them and tell them how they feel. When I ask the men in the group how many of them think that women are good listeners I rarely get more than one or two raised hands— usually I get none. When we have a concern, a problem to solve, or when we want to be understood, we choose people who will listen. Being one of those chosen few is a great asset for anybody.

<u>Listening is</u>:

The road to the heart.

The gate to the brain.

Growing in stature through the ears.

<u>Understanding is</u>:

The wealth of wealth
William G. Benham
Is not to prove and find reasons, but to know and believe.
Thomas Carlyle
Mutual praise.
Dorothy Parker
The soil in which grow all the fruits of friendship.
Woodrow Wilson

<u>Exercise #1</u>:

Listening and understanding are learned skills. This exercise will help you develop them.
1. Sit next to the person if at all possible. Try and keep any objects from separating you, i.e. a desk, a table, etc. This promotes camaraderie at work and closeness at home.
2. If it is appropriate to the relationship, hold the other person's hand. Even if you are angry with your spouse you need to hold hands. We have already discussed the power of touch. In this case holding hands says, "I may not be happy about the

situation but I still love or care for you." If hand holding is inappropriate but other "touching" can comfortably be used, please do so.

3. Make the decision that while the other person is talking you will use only these words in response: "I understand" or "I see how you could say that." You are not saying, "You're right, I'm sorry." What you are saying is, "I won't interrupt you, I am listening. Your opinion is important, you are safe to share your feelings with me; I care more about finding a resolution then I do about blame." Now that is a mouthful when the only words you are using are, "I understand" and "I see how you could say that." Even if at the time you do not understand, saying these words will help you to see the other person's viewpoint. This is the first step to effective resolution.

4. When this person has completely finished what he is saying (allow at least 15 seconds of silence) simply say to him, "I understand. Let me think about it for a few minutes." If he has more to say, listen and repeat the exercise until he has no more to add, then request time to think.

5. Leave the area for at least five minutes, but no more than ten. While you are gone do not make up a list of all the reasons the person is wrong. If you are angry that is fine, but you need to use this time to put yourself in the other person's shoes.

6. When you return ask him to listen to you

and let him know that you would appreciate no questions or interruptions until you are finished. When you are finished ask him to think about what you have said for a few minutes. Give him five to ten minutes and then return.

7. Then and only then look for a resolution, if there is still a need for one.

Controlling yourself in this situation will be one of the most difficult things you have ever done. When your boss has the gall to tell you that he thought you were rude to the client yesterday when he knows only half the story, it will be hard to say, "I understand." When your child is yelling at you because you went into his room without his permission it will be difficult to say, " I see how you could say that." It requires patience and tact to act with restraint when you think someone is wrong. The idea of placing blame has been ingrained in us. But think of two people standing on opposite sides of a wall. Each side is painted a different color and each color is the "right" color. The only way for each of these people to understand the color the other is viewing is to walk over to the other person's side of the wall...to examine the other person's point of view. Being right or wrong then is no longer an issue because each person can now see the other's side. This technique has repaired many broken marriages, partnerships and friendships. I have personally seen it bring brothers and sisters, parents and children, and employer and employee closer. It's worth it. The harder it is to perform these exercises, the more they should say to you that you haven't been listening in the past.

Facial Expressions

The index to joy and mirth, to serenity and sadness.

The face crowds a great deal into a little room. It is a reflection of the heart and the mind. Many people have worked since childhood to control facial expressions for that very reason. When you want to hide a thought or feeling you learn to control the face. This control can cause misunderstandings or it can eliminate emotional blowups. It is a quality the most dishonest and the most valiant of men share.

The main problem with facial expressions is that often we don't use them consciously.

You don't need to learn how to express emotion in your face. It is an instinctive action. The main problem with facial expressions is that often we don't use them consciously. We may be sad, but we tell an associate we are doing okay. He doesn't believe us because our face speaks otherwise. Therefore, you need to make the choice to either speak the truth or consciously adjust your facial expression. I am not going to give you any "shoulds" because there are too many different circumstances to consider. I'm sure you want a say so in what thoughts and emotions you share with others as well as when and where you share them. Being aware of your expressions simply gives you that choice.

Don't fool yourself that by <u>saying</u> your project is

34

going well it will be believed. Confidence, faith, and enthusiasm must be on your face or it won't be convincing.

One of the answers people have come up with to hide their thoughts and feelings is to teach themselves to portray a stone or poker face. They attempt to provide a blank canvas behind which actual thoughts are hidden. The observer can't decide what a person is really thinking. Be aware of the negative aspects of this poker face. It often conveys that you don't care about what people are saying, that you are bored, that you are afraid to tell the truth or even that you lack intelligence. Be careful where you use it. I would suggest that when your spouse is talking to you about something that upsets him is not a good time to wear an expressionless face.

The face animates the emotions and when your face displays a lively expression, it will make you a more interesting person to talk to and be with. In your profession you will be regarded as more enthusiastic and passionate about your work if you present an interesting face. If you work with kids at all using your face increases their interest tenfold. Don't take your facial expressions for granted. Whether you like it or not, your face is out there for all to see. You might as well make it a useful tool to build your world of success and happiness.

The Face is:

> *The best criterion of value.*
> > William Harlitt

> *Shorthand of the mind.*
> > Jeremy Collier

> *Doth testify what you be inwardly.*
> > Lewis Evans

> *The portrait of the mind.*
> > Cicero

Often a true index of the heart.

James Hovell

The title page which heralds the contents of the human volume.

William Matthews

<u>Exercise #1</u>:

Use just your face to answer the following questions. Hold each expression for five seconds. Don't move your head, use your hands, speak, or call on any other nonverbal movements:

What do you think of the state of the environment?
What do you think about our President?
When you think of your spouse how do you feel?
What does home mean to you?
Would you like to be in Tahiti right now?
If you saw a man strike your child what would you do?
Is education important?
How much weight would you like to lose?
Do you like animals?
What do you think about learning to sky dive?
Did you know that your blouse has ink all over it?
How do you feel about your work?
What is your opinion on the abortion issue?
How is your relationship with your mother?
...Father?
...Husband?
...Children?

Now do the exercise with someone else and see if you are understood. Words actually hinder the true meaning of your thoughts or feelings in many cases.

Exercise 2:

In front of a mirror, using just your face express the following emotions:
Aggression...Anger...Anxiety...
Apology...Arrogance...Bashfulness...
Bliss...Boredom...Caution...
Concentration...Confidence...Curiosity...
Demureness...Determination...Disgust...
Disapproval...Disappointment...Disbelief...
Distastefulness...Ecstasy...Eavesdropping...
Enthusiasm...Envy...Exasperation...
Exhaustion...Fright...Frustration...
Grief...Guilt...Happiness...
Horror... Hurt...Hysteria...
Indifference...Idiocy...Innocence...
Interest...Jealousy...Joyfulness...
Loneliness...Lovesickness...Mischief...
Misery...Negativeness...Obstinacy...
Optimism...Paranoia...Perplexity...
Relief...Sadness...Satisfaction...
Shock...Sheepishness...Smugness...
Surprise...Suspicion...Sympathy...
Thoughtfulness...Withdrawal

Options:

Try expressing these emotions to someone else and have her guess what you are communicating. Time it or limit the guesses to make it a game. Try it when you are in a strongly negative mood (such as angry, sad, lonely etc.). Do you notice a difference?

Body Language

I can tell more by a man's walk than ever his talk.
Anon.

Many times in history two different cultures have met and found a way to communicate by using body language or sign language almost exclusively. The body literally has a language all its own. It isn't important to know the theories and all the possibilities. All you need to do is to learn the common mistakes made and replace them with positive, successful ways to use this powerful form of communication.

Posture, gestures, movement and gait are the major parts of body language. This special language often is ignored as a means of communicating. Just because people don't come up to each other and say things like, "You sure have nice posture," or "I can tell from your gestures you're an energetic person," or "You certainly walk like you're someone to be reckoned with," does not mean that body language is not noticed.

Poor body language is more apt to be noticed by others. Slumping or slouching for instance will always be noticed and communicates either that the sloucher is self involved, not confident, sad, lazy, ashamed, unintelligent or even pathetic.

Positive body language can convey that you are self-confident, alert, intelligent, spirited, caring, happy, interested and honest. Your posture needs to be adjusted for the two major worlds in which you live, at work and at home. Often the posture we grew up with does not serve us well at work. The basic *listening posture* at work is to sit up straight (meaning hold your head and shoulders up) with your back resting against the back of the chair. Cross your legs at the ankle (not the knees); lay one arm on the arm rest of the chair if there is one and if not simply place your hands loosely in your lap. If you are on your feet while you are listening, then be sure to stand straight with your weight evenly distributed; keep your hands still without crossing them over your chest or clasping them— and limit your movement.

The basic *talking posture* for the work place is almost the same except that hand gestures and movements should be added. Return to your *listening posture* when the other person is talking.

Sitting or standing up straight communicates alertness, interest, confidence, intelligence, integrity and honesty. Sitting back in your chair with your arms and body relaxed communicates openness, understanding, graciousness and approachability. Crossing your legs at the ankle shows that you are professional and competent. When you cross your legs at the knee it changes your entire posture to one that is more sexy and less aware—a habit worth breaking at work. When standing it is best to limit movement as a listener to let the other person know you are attentive and are interested in what he is saying.

Clasping your hands conveys nervousness and says that you are more concerned with what you are feeling than with what the person is saying. Crossing your hands on your chest might be comfortable to you, but it is usually viewed as a defensive gesture by others. It is all right to add movement when you speak because it elicits interest from your listener.

Dorene is a confident, enthusiastic, intelligent woman with severe spinal curvature. When she came to me she was a little unhappy. The week before she had been in a heated discussion with an associate at work, and in anger the person said, "You're never happy anyway." Yet Dorene saw herself as happy and lively, and her associate's remark was quite a blow to her. We began to discuss posture and Dorene realized that she had become lazy about holding up her head as well as sitting and standing as straight as she could. Her associate may have construed her to be unhappy by the way she carried herself.

She made it a point to correct her posture at once. Although she suffered headaches and back aches for a few weeks, Dorene now tells me that correcting her posture has changed all her relationships for the better. Usually people don't say anything, so Dorene was lucky that she had been told. She literally didn't know what she was missing.

Posture in your personal life is much less structured and you should make sure that you are comfortable. The main thing to remember is that when you want someone to know you are listening sit or stand still and avoid clasping or crossing the arms. If you want to make a positive first impression the basic work posture already discussed is your best bet. As you become more relaxed with the person you are talking to you adjust naturally.

In addition to posture—in fact almost impossible to separate—are your gestures, movement and gait. If you wish to communicate that you are an outgoing personality your gestures and your steps when walking will need to be larger. Enthusiasm can be communicated by quick movement and step as well as use of the hands when talking.

Kindness or caring can be communicated strongly by gestures that are slower and less abrupt, movements that are open and inviting and a gait that is relaxed.

Control and organization are best expressed by precise gestures and movements along with a quick and direct walk. This is also the best gait for a woman alone in a possibly threatening situation.

One of the best ways to effectively use body language is to pick out someone you admire for a certain trait and then observe how she stands, sits, walks, uses her hands, moves etc. Look for the size and the speed of her gestures. You'll realize that her body language probably has a lot to do with the admiration you have for her.

You already know what body language means. You have used this knowledge unconsciously to make assessments of people all of your life. People have done the same to you. By becoming conscious of this skill you can be in better control of how others read you. If you want people to see you for who you are then become aware of what your body does. Use body language to your advantage.

The Body is:
> *Made for the soul to express itself.*
>> *Jean Mouroux*

Gestures are:
> *The last word in a conversation.*
>> *Anon.*
> *A much more enjoyable way to shout or whisper, especially for the listener.*
>> *Anon.*

Movement is:
> *The poetry of emotions and thought.*
>> *Anon.*
> *When the play of the body succeeds the play of the mind.*
>> *Anon.*

Exercise #1:

Decide on a trait you admire. It can be one you feel you already possess or one you wish to work on (honesty, professionalism, reliability). Next pick out a person who you admire for that trait. Observe and make note of the following:

••• What is the speed of the gestures?
••• What is the size of the gestures?
••• What specific gestures seem to be habit?
••• What specific gestures seem to be very effective?
••• Are the movements precise or grand?
••• Describe how she sits and stands.
••• Does her posture change during conversations?
••• Describe the pace of her walk.
••• Describe the size of her step.

After you have made your observations return to the original trait that you were interested in.Which of the above body languages do you feel best expressed that? Simply add those actions to your repertoire. Don't feel silly. Imitation is how you got all of the body language you already have. For further development you can either change to another trait or you can use the same trait and observe different people.

Exercise #2:

For this exercise use the list of words in Exercise 1 of the *Facial Expressions* section. Cover your face (a paper bag will work fine). Without the use of words or sound express with your body each of the emotions on the list. Have another person(s) try to guess what you are conveying.

Options:

Put each of the words on a separate slip of paper. Place the slips in a container and draw one at a time. Let the observers guess what emotion you are communicating.
Do it in teams like playing charades. Set a time and compete for who can get the most right.

Exercise #3:

With your group at work maintain a weekly anonymous suggestion box. Each week a particular person should be chosen whose body language will be commented on by members of the group who will report on individual slips placed in the box. Have each member of the group write down a gesture—movement, walk, posture—of the chosen person which he admires and what he thinks it says about the person. If there is any inappropriate body language mentioned it should be described on the back of the slip. Include what you think the language says about the person. Do not look for the negative. If it is not something that is glaring to you don't write it down. If you receive a negative comment about your body language, don't be upset. Think about the criticism and if you decide it is valid be grateful that it was pointed out to you in an unoffensive manner.

At the next staff meeting have the chosen person read off the positive comments. All other comments are to be for her eyes only. Encourage the staff to listen to all comments. It should be made clear that no one is required to make any changes in body language. This exercise is to increase awareness. Decisions made under duress generally aren't lasting. The decision to make changes is an individual choice.

Health, Fitness and Hygiene

Those who think they have not time for exercise
will sooner or later have to find time for illness.
Edward Stanley

Neglecting your health is the most thoughtless and selfish thing you can ever do to those who love you. Why is it that so many people expect their loved ones to take better care of them than they do of themselves? If you get a lung disease because of smoking, are you aware of the stress and worry you put on your spouse and kids?

If you have high blood pressure due to excess weight and have a stroke, do you honestly think it affects only you? If you are a parent who neglects her health, then you are teaching your children that taking care of themselves is unimportant. Children learn by what you do, not by what you say.

If you are a parent who neglects her health,
then you are teaching your children
that taking care of themselves is unimportant.

To others you are saying that you are not worthy of being loved or cared for. You are also saying that you lack confidence, love, esteem and appreciation for yourself. None of us means to be selfish and thoughtless but by assuming your health, fitness and hygiene affects only you, you are doing just that.

I was talking to a lady at a party who was very

upset with her mother for deciding not to have an operation for cancer that would extend her life. As she stood there chain smoking I asked her if she had children. When she answered, "Yes," I asked how her smoking was any different than her mother's action.

It's time to get off my little soap box and stress all the positive things that good health brings. Your good health is needed to be a winner, a success, to be happy and to enjoy life. A picture of health tells people that you are worth listening to, caring for, befriending—and just being around. Never will you meet a person in good health who is sorry for it. Give yourself and your loved ones the gift of making health and fitness a priority.

> *Give yourself and your loved ones*
> *the gift of making health and fitness a priority.*

You have the time and you can find the money. Give up other things if you have to. That's what priorities are all about. If you are a mother and think caring for yourself takes too much time away from your kids consider two things: By taking care of yourself you are teaching them to take care of themselves through example; you will be a more patient, giving, understanding, loving parent when you are with them.

It is so hard for me to stay off my soap box because I let my health decline at one point in my life and I have seen it diminish in people I love. It is so destructive. I had every excuse in the world not to work out and to eat however I chose to eat. Bad habits are not easy to break. That's why breaking them makes you a winner. If you still choose to continue with poor eating, little or no exercise, smoking, drinking etc., that really is your choice. It doesn't mean you won't be respected or loved, but it will diminish your health and it will eat away at good feelings you have about yourself.

It seems silly to talk about hygiene or cleanliness to adults but we all need a reminder. People notice dirty hair, unkempt nails, hands, clothes, face, and teeth, but they won't say anything. If you are a construction worker you are going to get dirty but are you that way when you arrive at work and do you stay that way when you get home?

Cleanliness is an extension of good health and it reinforces positive self esteem. Cleanliness is neglected by adults far more than it should be.

On your day off do you like to go without washing your hair? How about your nails? Do you ever let them "go" because you can't find the time? Have you ever taken a shirt out of the dirty clothes hamper and decided it was clean enough to wear again? Don't be embarrassed. Although not everyone has done these kinds of things, many people have.

First of all, it is important that it doesn't happen often. If you find yourself doing these things more than once a month, you need to consider what you are doing to your self esteem and the way others feel about you. When we want to make a good impression the first thing we do is get cleaned up. We feel better and, therefore, we do better when we are clean. Even if it is just a trip to the grocery store your dirty hair will make you feel worse about yourself. If you meet anyone you know it won't impress them either. When you are sick or tired getting cleaned up will make you feel, as my mother puts it, *like a new person.*

If you are one of those women who does everything

for everyone else and won't take time for your own health, fitness or hygiene at least don't confuse this decision with selflessness, kindness, sharing and giving. In fact it is just the opposite. Learn to give to the people you care about— take care of your health.

Health is:

> *The thing that makes you feel now is the best time of the year.*
>> *Franklin Adams*
>
> *Better than wealth.*
>> *Proverb*
>
> *A wise man ought to realize that health is his most valuable possession.*
>> *Hippocrates*
>
> *Life without health comes to be painful and oppressive to us.*
>> *Anon.*
>
> *No road that leads to health is either too arduous or expensive.*
>> *Michel de Montaigne*
>
> *Without health life is not life; it is unlivable.*
>> *Francois Rabelais*
>
> *Health and cheerfulness mutually beget each other.*
>> *Joseph Addison*
>
> *Beauty is not possible without health.*
>
> *Happiness lies, first of all, in health.*
>> *G.W. Curtis*
>
> *Cleanliness is a fine life preserver.*
>> *Anon.*

2

STYLE

Always the reflection of one's self respect.
Anon.

A person with healthy self esteem continues to grow and learn. One with weak self esteem may fight growth, but the first step is all it takes to create a chain reaction.

Being happy is a choice only you can make. There are many poor people who rejoice in life and many wealthy people who dread every minute of their days. You are in charge of making yourself happy. It is all up to you. I hope you chose to have your life be a wonderful experience. By making your nonverbal skills conscious and positive your journey will be easier and more enjoyable.

Nonverbal skills are like the shingles on a roof. No one is more or less important than the others, but the removal of any one will cause a leak. The effectiveness of the roof will be lost. Eventually, unless the shingle is replaced, the roof falls apart. Although working on a roof may not sound like fun, nonverbal repair is. We have talked about all the nonverbal "shingles" that lead to success except one.

The "shingle" that we don't yet have in place is how to "dress." Style is the *individual* manner in which you choose to express yourself. In order to have the choice of being seen as you wish it is necessary that you learn to dress for YOUR style.

The reason that learning about style takes longer than the other nonverbal skills, is that past teaching has often been incomplete, incorrect or inappropriate. Times have changed. Women have more opportunities and choices than ever before, but due to confusion in how to appropriately present themselves many women have lost both. We have had trouble finding a teacher.

---

*Style is the individual manner you choose
to express yourself.*

Historically, three avenues have been open to us to obtain appearance savvy. We could choose to follow fashion, business or give up completely.

The fashion world is expensive, temporary and often inappropriate for many women. Business doesn't make room for the individual and can therefore hinder your recognition for specific skills and talents. Choosing to give up may mean that you have let someone else—like your mother, friend, sister or clerk—"dress" you. It may also mean that you just wear "whatever."

Learning to dress in *style* is a fourth option. The remainder of this book is dedicated to giving you the necessary information to learn to project the image of your choice using style. This means an image that reflects *your* strengths and *your* advantages.

Your style reflects your personality. It is the best way to express who you are or want to be. Learning your style is having something to say and saying it as clearly as you can. Is it your style to be reserved or flamboyant? Would you like to be more sexy or classy?

When you dress in style you are recognized as being your own woman. You are also seen as being happy with who you are—a success—and admired even by people with totally different styles. Dressing in style means that if you want to communicate control—you do. If you want to communicate creativity—you do. If you want to communicate spirit, reliability, graciousness, caring, vivaciousness—you do.

Because the education offered on how to dress has been limited and prejudiced, we have developed many misconceptions. We seek out people who we think should know our individual needs and put ourselves in their hands. The problem is they usually know little or nothing about what we need and what is appropriate for our different worlds. It's like learning how to speak German from a person who only speaks Russian while you only speak English.

The two worlds in conflict—fashion and business—have made it difficult for us to learn about clothing. The fashion world has supported the rebel or "trend setter" ideal, while the business world has supported the role of the clone it labels the "professional." The problem is that both have taught what they want us to know, not what we need to know. The buzz words of "trend setter" or "professional" manipulate women into buying and wearing clothes that are inappropriate for them. A trend setter in Paris is different from a trend setter in South Dakota. A professional on Wall Street is different from a professional in marine biology. Business sees the rebel as dangerous. Fashion sees the clone as a conformist. So, which is the answer?

It is worthwhile to take a moment to better understand where these two worlds come from so that you can make better image choices in the future.

The Business World

When women began to step into positions of authority they followed the lead of the men. Women felt that in order to be successful they needed to imitate men in style and in manner. The problem with this was that the things that made women excel at managing other people were left by the wayside. Both men and women have recognized the error and the pendulum is swinging back.

Many courses in management training teach communication, caring, attitude, listening, team work, etc. The days of blind authority without leadership ability are coming to an end. With all of this wonderful movement in a positive direction why in the world do so many women maintain the old styles and mannerisms?

Usually it is because they think it is better to be safe than sorry. In this case if you are too safe you may even be sorrier. If you are conservative, organized, controlled and have little ambition then the "clone" way of presenting yourself might be just fine. But even so, there is more to you than that, and no one—not even you—will recognize or appreciate your differences if you don't project them. It is important to be professional and appropriate to your working world, but it is just as important to your happiness and success to be YOU. Learning to dress in style will give you both.

The Fashion World

This is a world of artists. Dramatic, off-beat, exotic, creative geniuses. Without the artists of the world we would be a boring species. That doesn't mean we would go to them for advice on how to do our taxes or how to repair a computer. Designing clothes and understanding how they fit into a certain lifestyle are two completely different skills. In looking for an answer some of us have turned to the fashion world against our better judgment. Somehow we think that by going along with what is "In" we can't make a mistake, because after all we didn't make the decision. But it is a decision to follow the advice of people who don't understand or relate to our needs.

Historically, the fashion world has told us when to wear black shoes and when to wear white ones. It has told us the colors, the lengths, the prints and the fabrics we should wear in order to be "In this season." Those days are no more. Women today have a lot of roles to play.

We go skiing, we run businesses, we nurse children, we clean house, we make love, we join organizations, and we volunteer to help others in need. Whichever role we play, those who live in a completely different world—as the designers of fashion do—can not help us decide what is appropriate for us to wear. You know better than anyone what your lifestyle is like. When you learn to dress in style you no longer need the fashion world to make your decisions for you.

The Elements Of Style

Dressing in style means that you are dressing for what is best for you. Being "YOU" may mean being conservative or it may mean being off-beat. Some styles include more fashion, others include more business, some have little of either. Style is what communicates all the strengths and advantages of who you are. It uses your definition of success, your desires, your needs, your talents and your personality.

Any style is simply the sum total of seven elements:

Proportion
Colors
Prints
Fabrics
Accessories
Makeup
Hair

Your preferences in each element define your style. For example, when it comes to prints do you prefer a large black and white polka dot or a pastel floral? Your preference is a reflection of your personality—therefore your style.

The following pages provide you with a more objective view of each of the elements of style. As a result you will be able to understand and discard misconceptions about clothing, style and dress. Common "Misconceptions" are actually listed in this section. You can spot the ones that apply to you and correct them.

At the end of each of the seven sections dealing on Elements of Style you'll be asked to answer questions designed to help identify your style. Each of the questions has nine choices. Each choice you make is registered on a tally sheet. The combination of your choices are what make your style.

Look at your style as a tapestry. Each Element of Style is like a thread in the tapestry. When any one thread is removed, forgotten, or woven incorrectly, a hole is created that will get larger if not repaired. In the past you may have lacked the threads necessary to weave the picture of yourself that you wanted.

After you learn about and choose the Elements of Style you prefer you will have the threads you need to create the beautiful, original, wonderful tapestry (style) of YOU!

Have a blast!

The Element Of Proportion

Done successfully proportion happens when each part of the body is dressed in order to flatter the whole figure. The most common mistake women make is to try to flatter one part of the body while ignoring what the effect is on another part or to the whole look. One of the more common examples is a woman with a small waist and large hips who wears a pair of jeans cinched tight at the waist and hugging the hips. The waist may look small but the hips look even larger than they are. When body proportion is off nothing is flattered. It's like bringing a bad piece of furniture into your home just to make a new piece look better.

Dressing in proportion communicates to others that you are successful (regardless of the cost of the clothes), intelligent, sharp, attractive, confident, decisive, and that you possess a healthy self esteem. Dressing out of proportion makes you look older, less aware, less confident and your clothes look cheaper. The most expensive dress you can find is not worth a nickel if it doesn't flatter you. Without good proportion no garment is flattering. Often women buy a garment because of the print or the fabric or the color. That is okay, but only if the proportion is right for your body. Proportion is the first thing you need to check when you buy clothes. If it's the wrong proportion don't buy it regardless of how many of the other elements of your style the piece fits. Well-proportioned clothes not only flatter your body but your purse as well. You will be able to mix and match almost your entire wardrobe. Your clothes will never—never—never go out of style and you won't have to have as many (unless of course you want to).

A big problem I have encountered when teaching

proportion is the misinformation mothers, sisters, friends, and clerks have passed on about the subject. Though these people may dress right for themselves, chances are their style and yours are not the same. Your opinion may be swayed by *their* favorite colors, lines, or fabrics, often with poor results. These people aren't wrong, only different.

Do you remember that outfit you bought that seemed perfect when you had it on in the store, but you rarely ever wear because there's something wrong? It was probably purchased based on someone's advice or the proportions were off. Also, you may have absorbed false information that characterizes you as "too short or too tall or too heavy or too cute for that." If you stay within the guidelines of proportion, your height, weight, leg length, hip size or nose shape will have nothing to do with what you can or can't wear. The most important lesson to be learned about proportion is that color, fabric, or any other element of style cannot compensate for bad proportion.

> *When buying clothes, always look at proportion first.*
> *If it is correct then, and only then go on to check*
> *the other elements of your style*

Do yourself a big favor. When buying clothes, always look at proportion first. If it is correct then, and only then go on to check the other elements of your style. If proportion is off forget that garment and move on. This rule will help to eliminate many pieces even before you try them on. Remember, proportion is the element of style that you never want to compromise.

Creating a well-proportioned look means paying attention to:

°°°Skirt (hem and fit).

°°°Jacket (lengths and fit).

°°°Necklines (type and fit).

°°°Sleeves (type and fit).

°°°Blouses, dresses and pants (type and fit).

These represent the places where clothing creates unnatural lines. The goal is to have clothing lines flatter your body lines.

SKIRT HEMS AND FIT

A correct skirt hem will create a complementary and attractive line for the hips, thighs, calves, tummy and overall body.

Why Is The Hemline So Important?

When you put the horizontal line of a skirt hem in the wrong place you can make yourself look squarer and stockier. My clients often use the word "frumpy." A $35 skirt in the right length is worth more and looks like it's worth more than a $150 skirt in the wrong length. What's "in" is what's best on you.

The Most Flattering:

There are three skirt lengths that give flattering body proportion. Which of the three you prefer will depend on your style.

°°° above-the-knee (mini).
°°°Classic.
°°°Long length.

Above-The-Knee (Mini):

Look at the shape of your knees. Find where the *thigh* starts to curve in to meet the knee. From that point and three inches *up* from that point is the range for this length. For an above-the-knee length this is the most flattering and the most practical. A straight skirt is the most trimming to the hips and thighs. A full skirt is good if you carry weight in the tummy, have straight hips and nice legs. (Refer to illustrations 1, 2, and 3.)

This is the best proportion for an above-the-knee skirt. It doesn't mean it is always appropriate. Regardless of what the fashion world says, a mini-skirt is sexy and therefore usually inappropriate for work. Even if "everyone" is wearing them, a skirt above-the-knee can hurt a woman in business.

The mid-knee classic length is recommended wear for business in place of the mini.

Classic Length:

Look again at the shape of your knee. Find the very bottom of your knee cap. From that point (*just* below the knee) to mid-knee is the classic length. This length should only be worn with a skirt that hangs straight down from the hips. Full and A-line skirts do not flatter in this hem length. (Refer to illustrations 1, 2, and 3.)

Long Length:

This time look at the shape of your *calf.* Observe how the calf muscle creates a "C" shape. The bottom of this "C" shape is the beginning of your long hem length.

From that point down to two inches above the ankle you are in your correct long length. Any style of skirt can be worn in this length. If your legs are so thin that there is no "C" shape, push the calf muscle forward with your hands to find the a "C." (Refer to illustrations 1, 2, and 3.)

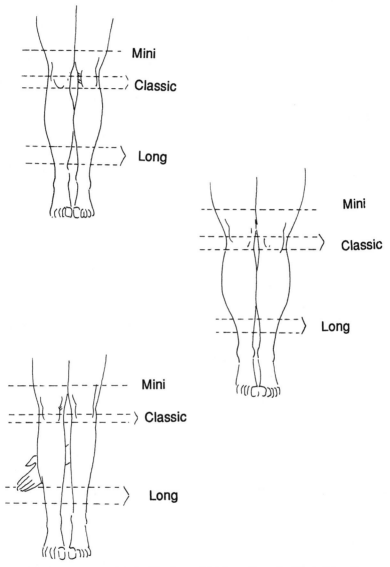

Illustrations 1, 2, and 3: Finding skirt lengths. 1. Mini. The line shows the shortest recommended mini. 2. Classic. Ranging from mid-knee to just below knee. 3. Long. Ranging from just below "C" shape of calf to two inches above the ankle.

The Exceptions

Do not make an exception with your hems. To have a skirt that flatters your body you must choose from the three hem lengths given. Hems that fall in any other area of the leg hinder your total look and throw proportion off. There are no advantages to wearing other lengths of skirts. You will not be able to mix and match your wardrobe; you will not be flattering your body; and you will go out of fashion with the seasons.

Misconceptions And Concerns

Misconception: A-line skirts are very practical and never go out of style

Actually A-line skirts are an example of what the fashion world designed for women to wear when they first entered the work force in suits. A-lines are not a good line for the body. Style should always be based on what is best on you. The A-line skirt is out of proportion and therefore is always out of style.

Misconception: Short women should never wear long skirts; they look silly.

The idea that short women can't wear long skirts is probably due to what mom taught you. But your personal style is the only thing that should make the difference in which of the three best hemlines you choose. Usually women under 5'4" have not tried wearing long skirts that are long enough. That's right *not long enough*. They often go into a petite store and the hem is brought up to the middle of the leg. This length is what makes a short women feel like she is wearing her grandmother's clothes. It also makes her body look boxier and shorter.

Misconception: My legs are too ugly to wear a classic length or above-the-knee length.

To be honest nine out of ten women who have said this to me have nice legs. They simply haven't been wearing their hem <u>short</u> enough. The truth is when you wear the hem line even one inch too long your legs will look heavier and out of proportion. Put on one of your skirts and look in the mirror and then hold it up at the proper length for the three hem lines. It's wonderful.

Concern: Do dresses follow the same hem length rules?

Yes, exactly the same.

Concern: I'm too tall to get skirts that are long enough to wear in my long hem length.

Long hem length is a problem for tall women and one that you will have to solve with patience or sewing. If you look long enough a skirt or a dress will pop up that is a long enough length. If you sew or want to go to a seamstress it may cost less and you'll get just what you want.

When you start getting compliments from people about how great you look, then you'll know that what you read here about hem lines was not only correct, but will improve your opinion of yourself.

Skirt Fit

A common reason for disliking a skirt fit is that the jacket worn with the skirt is the wrong length. You think the problem is with the skirt when it isn't. Following are simple rules for skirt fit:

1.	Wear one of the hem lengths described previously.

2.	If the skirt is tight around the waist get it altered. If you don't you will look heavier and the garment will lose versatility.

3.	A skirt waist band should allow you to put two fingers inside once it is fastened. This gauge is not just for appearance but for health and comfort as well.

4.	When a skirt tucks underneath the cheeks of your rear it is too tight. Such a tight skirt makes even the smallest buttocks look heavier. Also it doesn't help women with flat buns. A skirt tight in the butt makes the abdominal area appear larger.

5.	Your skirt is also too tight when it has creases across the tummy or hips before you sit in it. I know the fashion of today is to wear a skirt like a glove. This is a fad and I'd suggest allotting very little money to this notion. Glove-tight skirts will not mix in a wardrobe well and will soon become dated.

6.	Make sure all pleats lay flat across the tummy and hips.

7.	Your skirt should not hike up when you walk.

8.	You should be able to sit in your skirt without feeling like it is pulling at the hips or stomach.

9.	Elastic in the waistband is more comfortable and keeps blouses from coming untucked. When you learn how to accessorize correctly the elastic will not show.

JACKET LENGTH AND FIT

A good jacket length will create a complimentary and attractive line for the hips, stomach, thighs, buttocks, bust line and overall body.

Why Is Jacket Length So Important?

For the same basic reason that hems on skirts are important, so are hems on jackets. To put a horizontal line across your hips or stomach is to add weight to those areas. In addition, a jacket in any length other than the "most flattering" does not mix and match and dates itself quickly.

The Most Flattering

There are two jacket lengths (whenever I refer to jacket lengths I mean all cardigans and sweaters as well) to learn:
°°°Long length
°°°Short length

Long Length:
Find the bottom of your rear end. From that point down is your long jacket length. Be sure your jacket is completely below your buttocks. Even one-half inch up from that point will add weight to your hips, thighs, shorten your waist and throw off body proportion. How much longer below the buttocks you wish to go is only a matter of your personal style. The long jacket length can be worn with the above-the-knee skirt length, the classic length, the long length or pants. Jackets in this range are the most flattering and versatile jacket length.

Short Length

This length is right at your waist, or within one inch below it. The shoulders on a waist length jacket should be broad, soft and loose fitting. This style of jacket is to be worn with a skirt in the "long" length (see skirt hems) or a pair of pants. Which you prefer will vary with style. This is not as flattering to thick waists as the long style jacket.

The Exceptions

The peplum is a jacket that can be very flattering. Worn closed, this is a belted jacket that is most flattering when the shoulders are padded and the top is loose. It has its own skirt that reaches at least three inches below the beltline. It is most trimming worn with a long straight skirt and creates an "X" shape in the figure, showing off the waist and slimming the hips. (See illustration 4.)

Illustration #4: The Peplum Jacket: Peplum refers to the "skirting" below the belt on the jacket.

Misconceptions and Concerns

Misconception: The mid-hip basic blazer jacket is the most practical and best jacket for a working woman.

This jacket has the same problem as the A-line skirt. When suits were first made for working women they were an imitation of men's suits. We don't have men's bodies. Just because the shorter blazer has been in use longer does not make it better. It is less practical because it doesn't mix and match well with other things. The jacket is the most expensive piece in your wardrobe. Make it worth the money by wearing it more than one way. This can only be done by wearing the right length.

Misconception: Women close to five feet tall are too short for the long jackets.

They look beautiful in the long length of jacket. But *the skirt hem must be the correct length.* Try the long jacket with one of the classic skirt lengths first.

Misconception: Long jackets are for women who have weight to hide, not for thin women.

Even thin women like looking trim and showing off their sleekness. No matter what your body weight, the lengths given here will be the most flattering.

Concern: What about cardigans?

They should be measured the same way jackets are; either below the rear completely or right at the waist. Short cardigans should have shoulder pads.

Concern: What do I do with all my jackets which are the wrong length?

They should be your top priority to replace. One jacket in the right length is worth 20 in the wrong, no matter the color or fabric. Once you learn your style, the purchase of one jacket in the correct length can add dozens of outfits to your existing wardrobe. When you see yourself and hear all the compliments, you will no longer want to wear the other lengths.

Concern: What style of lapels should be worn?

This depends on taste. Lapels aren't dated in women's wear as they are in men's wear. It's the wrong length in the jacket that will date a woman's clothes.

Jacket Fit

1. Most women who wear their jackets too small are size two to size eight. The only reason I can think of for this poor fit is that retailers convince smaller women that tighter clothes show off their body. Not only is this not true but tight jackets appear to be of lower quality and older. Make sure your jacket isn't too small. Try on the jacket with a blouse. Push both the sleeve of the jacket and the sleeve of the blouse up to the three-quarters position. (Even if you don't intend to wear the jacket this way). If after pushing up the sleeves the shoulders, arms or back feel tight, the jacket is too small.

2. The front edges of the jacket should lay straight down from the middle of your breasts. If you are self conscious about large breasts, it will only make you look larger if you pull the fronts of your cardigans or jackets across your chest.

3. You do not have to close the button on the jacket just because the button is there. If the jacket lays correctly across the chest and shoulders it fits well.

4. Sleeves on your jackets are measured by having your palms facing and parallel to the floor with your arms at your side. The sleeve should rest on the top of the back of your hand. (See illustration 5.)

5. A double-breasted jacket is designed to be worn closed. If you are not going to wear it this way it is not a figure-flattering buy.

Illustration #5: The correct sleeve length for your jackets. The sleeve rests on the back of your hand when palm is facing floor.

NECKLINES

A good neckline will create an attractive, complimentary line for your face.

Why Is A Neckline So Important?

The right neckline lifts the eye of the beholder to

your face and especially your eyes. It thins the face area and lifts up the cheek bones, lengthens or shortens the neck and shows off the eyes.

The Most Flattering

Everyone looks good in a neckline that is higher at the back of the neck and lower in the front. (See illustrations 6 and 7.)

Illustration #6 and #7: The most flattering necklines are higher in the back and lower in the front. These are only two examples. There are many other styles.

The Exceptions

Neckline preferences will vary with style. The above guideline is for the most physically flattering.

Misconceptions And Concerns

Misconception: A buttoned-up collar is all that is appropriate for work.

This advice is just not true. Even the most conservative firms for which I have consulted do not find this neckline any more appropriate than many others. If you like to wear your collar buttoned up you should, but don't do it just because you think it is more appropriate.

Concern: I happen to love turtlenecks and jewel necklines.

There is nothing wrong with these necklines even if they are not higher in the back and lower in front. They are preferred by some styles.

Concern: I love low necklines. I have a nice bust line and like to show it off.

I think it is wonderful if you have an attractive bust. It's even better that you appreciate it. Learn what your bust line communicates about you when you choose to show it off. Choosing the appropriate time to flatter this asset can help your relationships at work and home. Reading the section on *Environment* will help your awareness.

Fit Of Necklines

The fit of your neckline is usually not a big problem. Just make sure it is comfortable and there is no pulling at the shoulders.

SLEEVES

A good sleeve length will create a complimentary

and attractive line for the waist, hips, bust, and overall body proportions.

Why Are Sleeve Styles And Lengths So Important?

The right sleeve provides an optical illusion that can slim the waist, hips and arms. It can make the torso look longer, less boxy and it can straighten slumped shoulders or diminish a gangly look.

The Most Flattering

There are four sleeve lengths to consider:
°°°Cap or sleeveless.
°°°Short sleeves.
°°°Three-quarter sleeves.
°°°Long sleeves.
The most flattering to the hips, tummy, thighs and body proportion is the three-quarter length. The types of sleeve you choose will vary with style.

Cap Or Sleeveless:

I would recommend this only for people who have either broad shoulders or a very trim torso, tummy and hips. A person with narrow shoulders will give the illusion of larger hips and thighs if she wears this style of sleeve.

Short Sleeves:

This length needs to be hemmed at an angle or rolled up to an angle on the arm. Try and stay away from sleeves that are cut straight across the arm. (See illustration 8.) Wearing a shoulder pad any time you wear short sleeves slims the hips and thighs. Be sure the sleeve is loose on the arm. (See illustrations 9 and 10)

Three-Quarter Sleeves:

The optical illusion that this creates is wonderfully trimming to the body from the waist to the knees. Adding a shoulder pad trims even more. (See illustration 13.)

Long Sleeves:

Wear this a fraction below the bone on your wrist. A sleeve a little long is okay; one too short should be pushed to three-quarters. A sleeve looks fine blousing over the cuff. A shoulder pad will help keep arms from looking gangly, will prevent the slumped shoulder look, lengthens the upper body and trims the lower body. (See illustrations 11 and 12.)

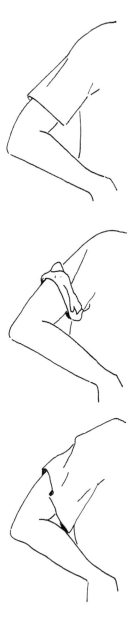

Illustration #8: A short sleeve cut straight across the arm gives a boxier and less flattering look to the body.

Illustration #9: Rolling a straight sleeve to create an angle trims the lower body and is less boxy.

Illustration #10: A short sleeve that is cut at an angle and is loose on the arm is the most flattering.

The weight loss illusion of sleeves and shoulder pads.

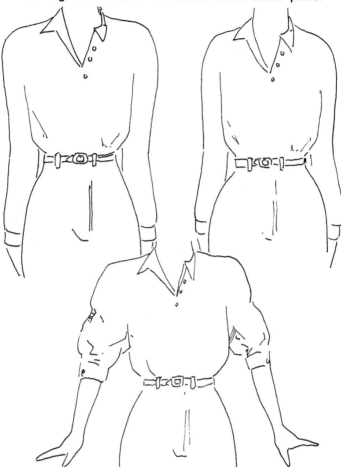

Illustration #11: Long sleeves with shoulder pads are trimming to the body and waist line.

Illustration #12: Without shoulder pads the body looks gangly, short-waisted and the hips, thighs and tummy look larger.

Illustration #13: The three-quarter sleeve with shoulder pads is the most flattering to a woman's body.

Exceptions

Although there are many varieties of design in sleeves, choose from the four lengths listed previously. Follow the general guidelines and you will have a flattering sleeve. The sleeves you choose to wear are a reflection of your style.

Misconceptions and Concerns

Misconception: Long sleeves are all that are appropriate at work.

It is true that a sleeve that reveals your under arm is inappropriate. A short sleeve longer than the middle point of your upper arm is fine and quite appropriate for most work environments. If it seems too casual, wear a jacket over it. Long sleeves create a more formal look and three-quarter sleeves a more open and communicative look.

Concern: How do I get my three-quarter sleeves to stay up?

Sleevebands are wonderful. (For more information see page 98.) You can also tuck sleeves under until they get snug and then push. Some of my customers use thick rubber bands for sleeve bands (be sure they are not too tight if you use them).

Concern: What if a top doesn't come with shoulder pads?

There are a lot of detachable shoulder pads available. My clients have always preferred the foam type that just slip in or those with a strip of velcro that attaches to the bra strap. (For more information see page 98.)

Concern: What exactly is a three-quarter length sleeve?

It's a sleeve that rests anywhere between the wrist and the elbow.

Concern: How come some short sleeves look good and others don't?

There are four reasons a short sleeve flatters (See illustration 10):

°°°The sleeve is loose on the arm.

°°°It is cut at an angle.

°°°It is worn with shoulder pads.

°°°The sleeve is closer to the elbow than it is to the shoulder.

Concern: I can see that three-quarter sleeves are more trimming but I don't like my jackets pushed up and I love long-sleeve blouses.

If that is part of your style you must make your decision accordingly. Don't completely rule out the three-quarter until you try it.

Fit Of Sleeves

1. Shoulders should not bind in the least across the back or under the arm. No matter what is suggested, this is not appropriate.

2. Cuffs on long sleeves should not bind. You should be able to easily move the cuff on your wrist.

3. All sleeves should be loose on the arm unless made from a stretch material. If the sleeves are short a loose sleeve is most flattering, no matter what the fabric.

4. If you plan on layering a piece be sure and try it on layered to check for comfort.

BLOUSES

Many women wear their blouses too tight. When you wear a blouse that is too small you will make the lower body look larger. It creates that "pear" shape that so many of us dread. More often it is smaller size women who do this. Be sure your blouses and tops are loose in the arms, shoulders and ribs. If you are wearing a knit fabric be sure it doesn't pull at the shoulder or under the arms. You do not need to do exercises in a blouse to see if it fits, but comfort is important. I suggest that you try on blouses one size up from what you normally wear to see the difference.

DRESSES

Fit your dresses like you would a skirt and a blouse separately. Consider the hem, neck and sleeve. A dress with a waist is the most flattering and most versatile. Jackets and cardigans go over this style of dress to create completely different looks.

PANTS

Pants should be comfortable. Make sure the pleats lay flat and not open. You should be able to put two fingers inside your waist band without holding in your tummy. Unless you want a sexy look, the pant leg should lay straight down from your butt, not tucked under it. Looking at yourself from the front, the hip line should lay smooth and not gather or hug. The rise should not bind at all. Hems on pants should lay softly on the top of your foot with one soft fold in the fabric on the leg. The back of the hems should be tapered one-quarter inch longer than the front. (See illustration 14.)

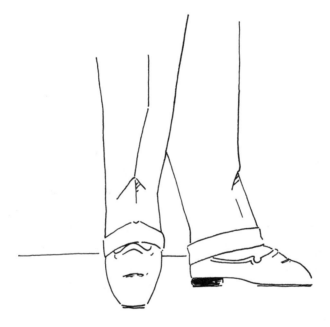

Illustration #14: This classic pant hem is timeless and figure
flattering.

USING PROPORTION TO OVERCOME
FIGURE CONCERNS

Let me preface this with a few facts and insights
into how women see themselves in our society.

Fact: Our culture and upbringing cause us to paint
a perfect picture of what we think we should look like.

Insight: Few women ever reach this picture. Those
who do usually feel lacking in other areas. Perfection is

impossible because it changes with the eyes of the person perceiving.

> *Accepting yourself for who you are adds more to your physical beauty than all the clothes and makeup in the world.*

Fact: We are taught not to compliment ourselves and to be modest.

Insight: This is destructive and causes each of us to always look for the negative in ourselves. To not say thank you when you are complimented is to negate the compliment. Compliments are a strong support for increasing self acceptance. When you negate compliments people stop giving them. In addition, it is an insult to negate a compliment for it is an opinion and therefore you are saying the opinion is wrong. Accepting yourself for who you are adds more to your physical beauty than all the clothes and makeup in the world. If self acceptance increases self love and leads to an increase in outer as well as inner beauty, why not try it? If you replace your negative statements with positive ones you will soon believe yourself. By looking in the mirror and saying," I am beautiful" you train your unconscious mind to believe it. Whether or not you are beautiful is all up to you. No one else gets the blame or the credit.

Listed below are the most common complaints and concerns from women about their figures. After each one I have written some ways to flatter these areas by using proportion.

Concern. I am too short-waisted.
Solution. To lengthen your waist you will want to

wear a belt that is close in color or tone to the top half of your outfit. If you are wearing a black skirt and pastel blouse then wear a belt that is a pastel or light color. (See illustration 15.)

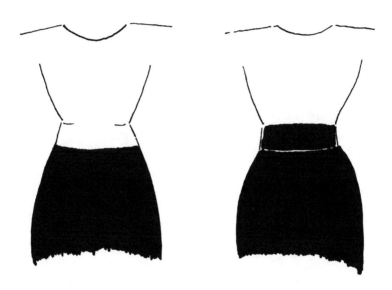

Illustration #15: Lengthening your waist. Wear a belt in the tone of the blouse, not the skirt or pant. This simple trick also slims a thick waist.

Concern. I have a thick neck, chin or puffy cheeks.

Solution. These characteristics can be helped by wearing a neckline higher in the back and lower in the front. Also a shorter hair cut with no hair below the jaw line. Earrings that dangle in the area of concern are not helpful.

Concern. My arms look gangly.

Solution. Don't wear long sleeves. Wear three-quarter sleeves. Wear shoulder pads and be sure the hems in your jackets and skirts are exactly right.

Concern. My rear, thighs, and hips are too big.
Solution. Wear shoulder pads, three-quarter sleeves, jackets in the right length, skirts in the right length and be sure that your blouses are loose fitting.

Concern. I carry all my weight in my stomach.
Solution. Wear three-quarter sleeves, all jackets and cardigans in the "long" length. Don't wear any tops that have excess fabric right at the tummy. When you tuck your tops in be sure to blouse them out a little. When you wear a belt be sure it blends with or matches the blouse and not the skirt or the pant. If you have thin hips and thighs try a short full skirt.

Concern. I'm too short/ too tall.
Solution. No you're not. You have probably been influenced by the ideas of what to look like fostered by this society. Start saying you are a wonderful height. Begin to dress for your style instead of dressing for false preconceptions.

Concern. My shoulders are too narrow.
Solution. Always wear shoulder pads and three-quarter sleeves, or angled short sleeves.

Concern. My shoulders are too broad.
Solution. Wear shoulder pads so that your shoulders don't extend past the shoulder seam of the garment. Oh, and say thank you. Broad shoulders are an asset. They thin the rest of your body.

Concern. I'm just too fat.

Solution. That's your opinion and you are entitled to it. Any woman, no matter what size, can be beautiful. It's all a state of mind. When you accept yourself as you are you will make the effort to look good now. Beauty is not dependent on dress size. Being happy with the way you look is a constructive gift to give to yourself. Don't use the excuse of excess weight to keep from looking your best right now. It is self acceptance that makes weight loss permanent.

CHOOSING YOUR FAVORITE PROPORTION

A. Which of the nine choices listed below would you most like to wear to work?

- A tailored jacket; with straight matching skirt; and a jewel neckline blouse in a contrasting color. (3)
- A duster (jacket that comes to the middle of the calf) with an interesting lapel; a pair of pants in the same color; a blouse or shell in the same color or in a print. (5)
- A fitted, solid-color jacket worn at the waist over a printed dress or skirt. (8)
- A jacket fitted to the hips with a snug mini skirt. (9)
- A long comfortable unlined, knit jacket, with a pair of pants and a cotton shirt. (2)
- An oversized textured jacket; with a long skirt in an entirely different material; a sweater or blouse of still another material; and boots. (6)
- A double-breasted blazer with matching dirndl skirt; a thin-striped basic blouse. (1)
- A jacket fitted at the waist; with a matching long flowing skirt and a high-neck blouse. (7)
- A mid-thigh length jacket with round shoulders; a drape neck blouse; and a long knife-pleat skirt the same color as the blouse. (4)

Make your choice and then write the corresponding number in the space provided on page139.

CHOOSING YOUR FAVORITE PROPORTION

B.   Which of the nine choices below would you enjoy wearing the most, even if you have never worn it before?

- A pair of sweats and tennis shoes. (2)
- A crisp cotton shirt and a pair of pants. (1)
- A long black skirt, oversized sweater, boots and scarf. (6)
- A cream wool suit, cream blouse and pearls. (4)
- A black wool gabardine suit with red blouse and gold jewelry. (3)
- A straight, magenta mini skirt with a matching blouse; a large black and white houndstooth jacket, long and with big shoulders. (5)
- A long rayon dress in a wine colored Victorian print. (7)
- A white lace, summer dress. (8)
- A mini dress, fitted to the body in an electric red glossy fabric. (9)

Make your choice and then write the corresponding number in the space provided on page139.

CHOOSING YOUR FAVORITE PROPORTION

<u>C.</u>   Which of the following would you most like to wear for a dressy evening out?

- A basic black dress. (3)
- A tea-length silk dress in purple or mauve. (7)
- A dark-colored skirt and a brightly-colored silk blouse. (1)
- A silk, loose-legged pant with a matching long cardigan. (2)
- A dress styled for a certain era (such as turn of the century or 1940's). (6)
- A brightly colored long sequined low-cut gown. (9)
- A dark navy dress with a stiff, white, lace collar and puffy sleeves. (8)
- A black silk pant with a gold, metallic knit tunic, huge shoulders and a great pair of black shoes with a gold accent. (5)
- A forest green, jewel-necked, knife-pleated silk crepe dress with diamond accessories. (4)

Make your choice and then write the corresponding number in the space provided on page139.

The Element Of Color

There is nothing complicated or confusing about knowing your best colors. If you like a color then you should wear it. Almost any color that you like can be found on the market today. When it comes to color there are two strong misconceptions. The first is that you should wear the colors that are "In." The second is that the colors you wear should be based on color analysis. Colors are a reflection of who you are and are the easiest way to project your style. Imagine a business suit in black with a red blouse. Now think of that same exact suit in soft pink with a cream blouse. The colors make all the difference don't they? Listen to yourself. If you love a color you should wear it.

What is "In" is what is good on you. Women no longer need fashion designers to dictate the colors they wear. In fact, if you decide to wear only the colors that are hot each season you can be seen as a follower, a rebel or inconsistent. If you love the fashion colors by all means wear them, just don't change every season simply because the garment industry is promoting something new.

> *Color is the easiest way to project your style.*

Then there is color analysis. You know the old defense: "Some of my best friends are..."? Well it is true that I have some very good friends in color analysis. But despite that fact, I still have to tell you that color analysis has done more harm to most women than good. When a woman pays for this service she is looking for something to make shopping decisions easier and to help her look better. Color analysis can do the former but is usually incomplete in the latter.

> *If you love a color you are going to look great in it.*

Color is one of the most powerful ways that you can express your personality. If you love a color you are going to look great in it. The reason one blue-eyed, fair-skinned, blonde wears soft pink and looks great in it and another person of the same coloring wears rust and looks good is that they like the color they are wearing. It expresses who they are. It really is that simple. The truly good analyst is the one who has education in the communication of color and she asks you questions about your life, dreams, goals, habits, hobbies, loves, hates, and career. Then she gives you a color grouping to reflect the beauty of you, not to match your eyes and hair. The color grouping is what makes your shopping easier and gives you mix and match strength in your wardrobe. All of your favorite colors should be included in any grouping. If you have had success with your color analysis it is probably because of the grouping. If the colors given you happen to be the ones you love, fantastic, but don't hesitate expanding into other colors you love.

Think back to your childhood. What was your favorite color? I guarantee that color is good on you. In your childhood no one told you that you were wrong and so you trusted yourself. Trust yourself again.

CHOOSING YOUR FAVORITE COLORS

Which one of the following color groups make you happy (not necessarily just to wear)?

- Neons and off-beat colors. (6)
- Electric pink, red and blue. (9)
- Clear primary colors . (2)
- The classics of black, red and white. (3)
- Dusty colored pastels or darks. (7)
- Pale neutral colors . (4)
- Soft pastel colors . (8)
- Basics such as navy, gray, beige. (1)
- Jewel tones and black. (5)

Make your choice and then write the corresponding number in the box provided on page 139 .

The Element Of Prints

Prints, like colors are very personal. If you love a print then it is the right one for you. Try not to let anyone talk you into a print. Don't buy a print just because of the colors or because it seems more appropriate. The prints you are drawn to are always appropriate—for you. Because prints are so personal you will get a large variety of responses from people. Your weight and height have nothing to do with the size of the print you can wear (again, it is proportion that is important).

CHOOSING YOUR FAVORITE PRINTS

Which of the following prints would you most like to wear?

- Checks, plaids or small dots. (2)
- Geometrics, paisleys and florals which are bright, bold or large. (5)
- Small florals, thin stripes and ginghams. (8)
- Mixed prints such as flowers with geometric or antique floral with menswear stripes. (6)
- Animal prints or bright abstracts. (9)
- Victorian and antique prints. (7)
- Small paisley, geometric, or houndstooth. (3)
- Mostly solids, only prints that are very subtle and don't have drastic color variety. (4)
- Glen plaids. (1)

Make your choice and then write the corresponding number in the box provided on page 139.

The Element Of Fabric

Fortunately there has not been a lot of bad teaching in this element just bad experience. Rayon, once the horror fabric comes in all kinds of wonderful textures now. Not all rayons water spot or wrinkle terribly anymore. This is a great fabric and even comes washable as well. If it has been a while since you tried rayon you might consider it again. If you feel more comfortable with assurances, simply ask the merchant you are dealing with to write a guarantee on your receipt that it won't waterspot or wrinkle horribly. It is true that linen and some cottons wrinkle. Whether or not the wrinkles bother you is a matter of style. I would seriously question anyone who said, "This linen doesn't wrinkle."

If you ask about the care for a garment and the answer the clerk gives you contradicts the manufacturer's care label, be sure and get it in writing. If the merchant is offering suggestions but doesn't wish to put it in writing, then you need to take full responsibility for the care of a garment.

Silk and gabardine wool are probably the most misunderstood fabrics. Both of these are natural and if not blended with another fiber have great breathability. If you hang a garment made of silk or wool so that air can flow through it, body and environmental odors will usually disappear. You do not need to clean these fabrics a lot. The chemicals in dry cleaning are not good for any of your clothes. Over-cleaning natural fibers breaks down many of their attributes. After you wash silk I always suggest rolling it up in a damp towel and putting it in the freezer for about an hour. Remove it and press with a warm iron.

This "pops" the silk out and makes it like new again. If you are concerned that a bright washable fabric may fade put some white vinegar in the water with it and wash it by itself the first time. I don't recommend using the supermarket detergents made for "fine washables." Instead buy a product from a boutique that is made for fine, delicate fabrics. There are few, if any, astringents and chemicals in these products that can harm your fine things. Baking soda is a wonderful product to release odors.

For the sake of our environment always try to buy no-phosphate detergent; it cleans just as well and rarely costs more.

CHOOSING YOUR FAVORITE FABRICS

Which one of the following do you like the feel and the look of the most?

- Fresh lines with crisp lace, organza and voile. (8)
- Body hugging fabrics such as knits, lamé, and satin. (9)
- Sleek lines with raw silk, crepe, and cashmere. (4)
- Oversized clothes with heavy cotton, gauze, wide wale corduroy and coarse textures. (6)
- Crisp lines with cotton, denim, and cotton flannel. (2)
- Clean lines with wool flannel, tweeds, and oxford shirts. (1)
- Angular lines with suede, linen, and jacquard. (5)
- Defined lines with silks, wool gabardine, and crepe. (3)
- Flowing clothes with silk, rayon, chiffon, and sheer wool. (7)

Make your choice and then write the corresponding number in the box provided on page 139.

The Element Of Accessories

No element of style defines you better, gives you more versatility in your closet, helps you look more together or is as much fun as accessories. What size to wear, how to wear, when to wear, with what, how to combine accessories, all are considerations that women have had to handle in the past on a hit or miss basis. Accessorizing is a mystery to many women. Some women continue to buy mistakes and some just give up. Believe it or not how to wear and choose accessories is logical and quite easy as well. In jewelry you can wear any metal, regardless of your coloring. Preferences are based on style not on your skin or hair color. There are some excellent quality costume jewelry companies such as Monet or Napier. But keep in mind that no accessory will correct an outfit that is in the wrong proportion. Accessories are the biggest money saver in your wardrobe when used correctly and the most costly when worn only one way and with one outfit. Using the magic of accessories to look better and save dollars is not only smart, it's fun.

Even my clients who came in expressing how much they hate to shop have found accessories the area they most enjoyed. An $80 belt that helps you to create ten outfits with the clothes you already own is worth every penny. A $15 belt that is worn with only one outfit is worth much less. On page 107 you are given ten ways to combine accessories in order to complete an outfit or a look.

95

UTILITY ACCESSORIES

There are a few accessories that are utility pieces. These are things we typically use anyway (or would find helpful to use). Unfortunately, they seem to be over-purchased or neglected completely. They include: nylons, shoes, purses, shoulder pads, sleevebands.

Nylons. This is golden information and will make a huge difference in your look. The traditional hose (the skin or suntan color of nylons) fail us in supplying what we want. The only time you want to wear a skin or suntan color of nylon is if you want to achieve a sexy look. What is unfortunate about this color is that many women view it as conservative when in fact it draws attention to the leg by giving it a nude look. Nylons should assist rather than hinder your look. The wrong color of nylon changes your entire appearance.

> *Wear nylons that are the same tone as the hem of your skirt, dress or pants.*

For a finished, feminine, appropriate, classy, professional look that makes your clothes look of higher quality, you will always want to wear nylons that are the same tone as the hem of your skirt, dress or pant. The best natural look is no nylons at all, which is inappropriate at work. For the dark hemline—wear off- black or charcoal hose. For the light hemline—use silver- gray or cream hose. By dark I mean colors such as dark- brown, black, navy, forest-green, burgundy and jewel tones. Light means colors such as white, taupe, light-gray and pastels.

If the color of your hem seems to fall somewhere between this description of dark and light then use one of the gray colors of hose (charcoal or silver gray). The idea is for the nylon to carry the tone of your outfit down to the floor. There is no need to match your hem with the same color of hose (navy dress, navy hose) although some styles do like to do this. However, if you never buy another pair of hose other than the four suggested here, you will always look great, be appropriate, and save money as well.

Shoes. Match the tone of your shoes with the tone of your nylons. You do not need to have shoes that match your clothes or other accessories. If your hemline is dark the nylons are dark and the shoe is dark. Black or navy (for dark) and taupe or gray (for light) are all you ever <u>need</u> to own in flats and pumps. These are basics that all styles should have. Shoes that are closed all around and a flat to medium heel are best for work. A heel above two inches becomes sexy in appearance.

Purses. Again you need only concern yourself with tone. If your outfit is dark, carry a dark purse; if it is light, use a light purse. Black or navy, taupe or gray are the basics to have. Textures and multiple colors are best if tones are alike.

> *If your outfit is dark—carry a dark purse;*
> *if it is light—carry a light purse.*

Shoulder Pads. Shoulder pads trim the lower part of the body and add style to every outfit you wear. You may think you don't need padding if you have broad shoulders, but without them you will lose some of the finished look and those broad shoulders won't be shown off. Don't worry about shoulder pads going out of fashion. As long as women want clothes that slim or add quality to their appearance shoulder pads will stay in style. The fashion world threatens that shoulder pads are going out, but smartly dressed women have continued to wear them. If your favorite store doesn't have any detachable shoulder pads ask them to contact *Stay Put* or *Silhouette.*

> *As long as women want clothes that slim or add quality*
> *to their appearance shoulder pads will stay in style.*

Sleevebands. These are a fairly new accessory and are used to keep your sleeves at three-quarter length comfortably. You can get them at most boutiques. If your favorite shop doesn't have sleevebands ask them to contact *BettyJon's of Dallas* for you.

FINISHING POINT ACCESSORIES

The other important accessories are the ones that are used to create new looks, finish your outfits and define your style. The "finishing point" accessories are:

Earrings: Look at the iris (the colored portion) of your eye. That is the size of the smallest earring you should wear. For most people this is about the size of a dime or nickel. The size of the orbit of your eye (the bones that encircle the eye) is the largest earring you should wear. Some women question these parameters, but the purpose of an earring is to flatter the eye and face. If you wear an earring smaller than suggested it isn't accentuating anything. If you wear an earring larger than suggested it detracts from your face and eyes.

Dangling earrings are designed for fun. In addition they draw attention to an erogenous zone and so can be too sexy for many situations. The best dangle is one that has some volume to it and isn't pencil thin. A fish hook style often draws the observer's eyes downward and accentuates the jaw and neck. Your height and weight have nothing to do with the size of earring you should wear. It is your eye size and individual style that determine this.

If you are allergic to some metals call local jewelers or boutiques and ask if they carry a liquid plastic or acrylic product that you can apply to the jewelry. There are several such products on the market available. These last longer and work better than fingernail polish. Pierced earrings can be converted to clips and visa versa. Ask your favorite boutique for this service. Many already have it. You can also find the converters at craft stores and convert the earrings yourself.

Necklaces: A 16-inch necklace is not versatile and is best worn inside a collar that is open at the neck. This length shortens the neck and can add weight to the jaw, chin and neck.

An 18-inch necklace is an awkward length and yet is the most popular one sold, especially as fine jewelry. It is too short to stay outside most collars and too long to be visible inside. If you have a nice gem stone you want to show off try wearing it on a longer chain. The 18-inch length is also too short to flatter the jaw, chin and neck.

The 24-inch necklace is the best basic size and all women can wear it. It fits well with collars and is versatile. If you like small jewelry pieces you will not want to go for a shorter length than 24 inches. This length creates a "V" look at the neck, accentuating the face. This is one of the two lengths recommended for your basic accessory wardrobe.

A 30-inch necklace is the second most versatile and flattering length of chain. If it falls between your breasts or won't lay open, or if it is within two inches of your waist then it is too long for you. This length doesn't have to be bold.

Longer than 30 inches is always dramatic and can be worn successfully—considering the above advice.

Brooches _(pins)._ A brooch can be feminine, dramatic, or tailored. You can add an incredible number of looks to your wardrobe when you learn to wear brooches. They aren't just to be worn on outer coats or lapels. A pin at the shoulder is beautiful for evening. It is a great way to finish off a plain blouse or dress. At the neck, shoulder, lapel, or on a belt, a brooch is a variety piece. From very conservative to exotic, this is an accessory you should add to your wardrobe.

When you attach a brooch or pin, wiggle the point of the pin into the fabric. Don't poke! When you remove the brooch, rub over the hole and it will close. Poking tears or pulls the threads, leaving holes.

Pins always look different and more tailored when they are attached to a garment. The colors in the piece often pick up those in the clothes. The size of the pin should be at least as large as a silver dollar. If you have a lot of smaller pins try clustering them together. Button covers fall into the same category as brooches. Some styles will wear pins more than others, but they are a part of all styles. Brooches are second only to scarves in versatility and practicality.

Scarves: In Europe women have always worn scarves. They don't spend as much money on clothes as we do, but they want to get as much variety out of their wardrobe as possible and still be in style. The use of scarves are their secret.

Scarves are the most misunderstood and under-used accessory in the United States. There is no reason at all for scarves to be complicated. Once you learn how to use them you will be amazed at what they can do for your wardrobe. There are two advantages to scarves:

1. They extend or update clothes you already own.
2. They add variety and individual style.

Women who have told me they don't like scarves are in the majority. Once a woman learns how simple, elegant, cost-saving and fun scarves can be her attitude almost always is changed.

I tell most of my clients not to use a mirror when putting on a scarf. The mirror causes them to fuss and try for a "perfect" look. The fabric is the key to a good scarf and each fabric lays a little different. I am going to give you a few ways to wear a scarf. (See illustrations 16 to 20.) There is no reason to learn any other ways. If you do want to experiment go into a store that carries scarves and ask a clerk to show you. Don't worry if you can't follow a book on scarves, I teach about scarves and I can't either. A scarf will make more wonderful outfits out of what you buy and already own than any other item in your entire wardrobe.

FIVE WAYS TO WEAR SCARVES

Illustration #16: <u>Rubber Band Design.</u> Turn your scarf backside up. Grab some fabric and wrap a rubber band around it. The band will need to be doubled for tightness. Turn the scarf around and you have a design. To wear, simply tie behind your neck. A fancy knot isn't necessary. Any shape of scarf can be used.

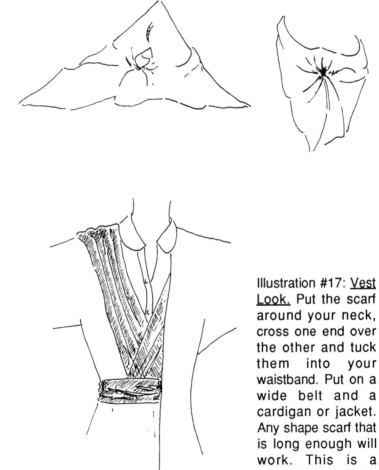

Illustration #17: <u>Vest Look.</u> Put the scarf around your neck, cross one end over the other and tuck them into your waistband. Put on a wide belt and a cardigan or jacket. Any shape scarf that is long enough will work. This is a wardrobe-stretching technique.

Illustration #18: Cowl-neck. Fold a triangular scarf into an oblong and wrap the scarf around the neck to create a high, cowl-like collar. Put one end of the scarf under the cowl and one over. Tie the ends together.

Illustration #19: Necklace-look. Fold a square or triangle into an oblong shape. Tie ends so that the scarf is necklace length. A brooch pinned to the side adds a nice touch.

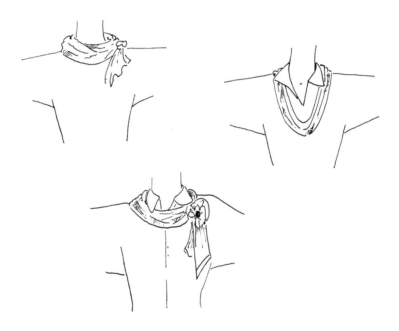

Illustration #20: Draped Scarf. Lay a scarf of any shape asymmetrically around your neck. The shorter side should be no lower than your breast. Grab the longer side—about two inches up from the bottom. Continue to grab fabric about every six to eight inches until the long end is at about the same height as the short end. Using a brooch or scarf pin, attach the two ends by bringing the long one over to the short. Let the ends hang down on one side.

Belts. Nothing finishes your outfit better than a belt and I recommend them for all sizes and shapes, even if you carry your weight in your stomach and abdomen. Belts are a great accessory to enhance your figure. One great style of belt is the raw silk velcro wrap that costs about $16.00. If your favorite boutique doesn't carry velcro wrap belts ask them to contact *Las Manos* or *Jan's Originals* as sources for them.

Bracelets. Bracelets don't have to be large or noisy unless you want them to be. A chain bracelet is beautiful and feminine and less cumbersome than a watch. If you wear a watch, the bracelet watches are wonderful. If you want to wear a basic watch as a bracelet just buy a chain bracelet and wear it on the same hand as the watch. A watch is not considered to be a finishing accessory unless worn as a bracelet. Bracelets can be a terrific accessory to add to a casual outfit.

Shoes Of A Different Color. This idea is not for every style, but it can look great when done properly. If you are wearing an outfit that is virtually the same color from shoulder to hemline and if you are wearing nylons the same tone as the hem, then simply put on shoes of a different color. Don't pick up the shoe color in a belt. Instead, pick it up in an accessory up at the neck. Matching shoes, belt and earrings should only be used if you want the look of the 40s and 50s. An example would be a black dress, dark nylons with a magenta shoe and necklace.

Printed Clothing Above The Waist. The print is the accessory. Keep this in mind when deciding the number of finishing point accessories you want to wear.

How Many Finishing Point Accessories Should You Wear ?

The number of finishing points you use will depend on your style of dress. Following is a guide:

One large finishing point is effective if worn at the ear or neck—this adds flair to casual or dressy outfits.

Two finishing points are used for a casual look.

Three finishing points are used for a professional or classy look.

Four or more finishing points are used for an artistic or dramatic look.

For more specific information on the suggested number of finishing points look at the end of the Accessories Wardrobe for each style.

TEN WAYS TO ACCESSORIZE ANY OUTFIT

By using "finishing point"accessories you can create countless outfits. Here are ten popular ways:

1. Select a neck piece (necklace, pin, scarf), then take any color in the neck piece and wear it in a belt. *Option:* Add a *basic earring or an earring of a color found in the neck piece. You can make an existing wardrobe look new simply with correct proportion and this accessory technique. Get a friend and go to a local department store and play with putting different tops and bottoms together simply by using accessories in this way. You will be surprised. **You are creating designer looks without the designer price.** It always, always works. This is the only method you'll ever need to learn to become a wizard with accessories. But if you do want to learn more, go on reading.

2. Select a multi-colored belt. Take any color in the belt and wear it in an earring. *Option:* Add a *basic bracelet.

3. When wearing a jacket, match the color of the jacket with a belt. (This ties your jacket in with a lot of your clothes.) Wear a *basic or different colored earring. *Option:* Add a *basic necklace, bracelet or brooch. *Or:* Add a necklace, bracelet or brooch in the color of the earring.

4. Wear a combination of any two pieces of *basic jewelry. All necklaces must be at least 1/4 inch thick for this method. *Option:* Wear a combination of any three.

5. Button up your blouse to the neck and put on a brooch. Put on a 30-inch necklace or longer in a metal or stone found in the brooch. *Option:* Wear a *basic earring or

one that matches the pin.

6. Wear a gem or stone on a 24-inch chain. Match the earrings to the stone or wear a *basic earring to match the chain. *Option:* Add a *basic bracelet or one of the same stone. Keep the size of the jewelry all close to the same scale as possible. *Or:* Add a belt in the color of the stone.

7. Wear one strong finishing point that is noticeable at the ear or neck. This is a great way to wear the huge shoulder duster earrings.

8. Wear a print in a dress or a blouse. Add a *basic earring. *Option:* Add a *basic chain, brooch or bracelet. *Or:* Add a belt of a color found in the dress or blouse.

9. Wear a neck piece in the color of your pant or skirt. A great example is cream with pearls. *Option:* Add an earring of the same color

10. Wear a combination of solid colors in your clothing and put on a totally different color of earring. Wear a belt that matches the earring. *Option:* Add a simple necklace in the same color.

* "Basic jewelry" varies and is identified in the accessory wardrobe for each individual style. Once you choose your "core" style, you'll discover your basic jewelry.

CHOOSING YOUR FAVORITE ACCESSORIES

Which of the following would you most enjoy wearing?

- No accessories at all. (1)
- A simple chain of gold or silver. (2)
- A big fringed scarf. (6)
- A wide, fun belt. (5)
- A soft scarf at the neck. (7)
- A bow-shaped pin. (8)
- Pearl necklace and earrings. (4)
- A classy watch. (3)
- Drop swinging earrings. (9)

Make your choice and then write the corresponding number in the box provided on page 139.

The Element Of Makeup

Makeup is a simple thing made very complicated by the fashion world, the entertainment world and the cosmetic industry. The entertainment world is populated by celebrities who have to be prepared for the unexpected photo;they're always in the limelight. An entertainer's makeup is a part of her costuming. On the other hand, most of us have to deal with people face to face within a few feet, not on stage or in front of a camera. We need makeup that makes our skin, eyes and facial features look good. We don't need to show off makeup. We need it to show us off. Makeup, when applied correctly, is not meant to cover up, it is meant to highlight features you love and diminish those you don't. Applying makeup skillfully is not a difficult art to learn. You just need to forget everything you ever learned before.

Makeup applied carefully creates the illusion that you don't wear any. Regardless of your past experiences using makeup is important to look and feel your best. It really is easy. Only eight percent of all the women who have come to me over the years did a good job at applying makeup. I had the wrong idea of what makeup was all about myself. It became clear when I saw a "naturally" beautiful woman with her makeup off. She had good features, but it was makeup and how it was applied that gave her the "natural" look. It was obvious that the real art is not to paint the face. It is to look as if you have no makeup on at all.

Give yourself permission to forget what you think you know about applying makeup and you will learn a lot. Even if you have always loved makeup and think you have it under control you will learn some new things.

Using too much makeup is the biggest mistake a woman makes. Not wearing any at all is a close second. With very few exceptions, a woman is judged as cheap, unhealthy, unclean or silly looking when she uses too much makeup. This is a universal interpretation and few women want such a negative reaction. Most women who go without makeup have been to a professional makeup artist...or two or three...and have had nothing but bad experiences. A woman goes to a professional because she wants to look better. Instead, she often leaves feeling as if she is wearing a mask that needs to be washed off immediately. Makeup done well gives you a finished and complete look, like doing your hair or wearing shoes.

Another major misconception some women have is that they need to change their makeup to match their clothes. Makeup is not to show off clothes, it is to show off you. If you want a dramatic, exotic or sexy look, any other element of style will serve you better. The only color in your makeup that should ever change is your lipstick.

EVERYTHING YOU EVER NEED TO KNOW about using makeup to look your best is here on these pages.

If you apply makeup as taught here you will look more attractive, more beautiful, more finished, more alluring, healthier and younger. This is accomplished by showing off your eyes, skin and other facial features.

Skin Care

Skin care is the most important part of your makeup because nothing covers up bad skin. You may think that heavier makeup covers a poor complexion but usually it just sends up a flag that you are trying to hide something and it isn't hard to see what. Skin care is simple, easy and vital to your beauty and health. Your skin is an organ of your body and it defends you against the environment on a daily basis; it needs your help. Cosmetic companies spend a lot of money on packaging and advertising rather than on producing the best product for your skin. If a product is heavily advertised I would shy away from it.I suggest you buy one of the lines sold by representatives in home demonstrations. Since there are poor products here as well, it is worthwhile to know what to look for. The points listed here will serve as a guide:

A. There should be no mineral oil in any of the products, including the foundation. Many will try and tell you that they use only the finest mineral oil. No mineral oil is fine enough for your skin. Others will tell you that it is controversial as to whether mineral oil is bad for you or not. As a rule mineral oil is used in the products these cosmetic merchandizers are selling. If you have tiny bumps on your skin it is probably due to mineral oil in your lotions or skin care products.

B. Make certain that the products you buy do not promise to get rid of wrinkles or to create a rapid change in your skin.

C. A quality line of skin care products will offer a cleanser, a rinse (if the cleanser is not removable with water), a moisturizer and an exfoliate to sluff off dead skin cells. The moisturizer should be light and not oily.

Do not use skin care products from one line with

those of another. They are not formulated the same and many skin types have adverse reactions by mixing various brands of products.

D. Make sure there is no alcohol in any of the products, including the foundation and the rinse.

E. Be certain that the exfoliate (mask) has clay, mud or egg in it and can be removed with warm water and a cloth. Peel and scrub masks are too harsh, can damage the skin and do nothing that a warm water mask won't. If there is no mask in the line be sure that there is a product that takes off dead skin cells without scrubbing or peeling.

F. Require a statement in writing that you will get a full refund if you have any reaction to the products you purchase.

G. Make certain that there are no hormones in any of the products.

H. The products should be easy for you to use so that you will use them everyday.

I. I suggest you discover if the company tests its products on animals. You may have some strong feelings about protecting the innocent. I do, and I thought I'd mention it.

J. If the product you buy lives up to these guidelines, it is of good quality. Make sure that you don't settle for less than the best. Check out the new formulations of Nu Skin, Shaklee, Mary Kay and Nouvier products.

Foundation:

Foundation is not to cover up your skin. It is to even out the tone. It should not be heavy or greasy. It should not have a yellow cast to it (regardless of your coloring) because it will age you. It should be an extension of your skin care, feel good and be very easy to put on. A good foundation is one that blends so easily that it could be applied without a mirror and look great. Foundation should never show lines where it stops and your skin starts. The foundation is not an item with which to add drama to your face. A good foundation gives you a smooth blank canvas to begin with, but it will never cover up wrinkles or bad skin (something that can be done in a photograph). You may very well feel pale when you apply a good foundation because it will have taken out redness and splotches in your skin. That's a good sign; color comes later.

To find a foundation that is light, comfortable, good for your skin and doesn't have yellow in it is hard but don't settle for less. I have done thousands of faces and yet use only two colors of foundation. One shade is for most African-Americans and the other is for everyone else. I use the foundation made by *Shaklee* and 100 percent of my customers love it. The company offers a lot of shades but all you need is "mocha" if you are African-American and "ivory" if you aren't.

Eye Shadow:

Eye shadow should not be seen nor should it be an attention grabber on your face—it is to shadow the eye, to give it definition, to show it off. The main mistakes we make with shadow is not blending it properly and wearing too many colors or the wrong colors. The only colors you ever need to wear, regardless of your coloring are gray, brown, skin color (your skin) and possibly very light pink, dark teal or deep purple. Brown deepens the color of the eye; gray softens it. Teal emphasizes the brown in the eye and purple brings out the green. The brown and skin color should not be of a yellow cast at all. Brown needs to be the color that you had in your crayons as a kid. Get rid of any colors with yellow in them. Yellow colors make the whites of your eyes more yellow and create a sallow and unhealthy look regardless of what you may have been told in color analysis. Get rid of any bright or pastel colors. Do away with cream shadows and go to the powders. I realize that limiting your colors is one of the toughest things to do. You'll be glad you did.

Eyeliner:

The fashion world is trying to push liquid eye liner back into makeup. I hope you choose to ignore this. The purpose behind eyeliner is not to show off how straight a line you can draw. It is to open up, highlight and lift the eye. Any eyeliner on the top lid will make your eyes look heavier and smaller. Eyeliner on the inside of your eye makes your eye look smaller and often beady. Thick eyeliner surrounding the eye has a "cheapening" look to it. A dark liner can have the same effect on the observer. Too much eyeliner ages the wearer and shows off the wrinkles around the eyes.

The only colors you ever need are gray, navy or brown. Black should be used only if you have dark hair, skin and eyes. Gray softens the eyes, navy makes brown eyes browner and blue eyes darker. Brown looks natural and thickens the look of the eyelash; it enhances the color in blue eyes. Black isolates the eye from the face unless used by someone with dark hair, skin and eyes.

Eyebrow Pencil:

This should be used only to darken brow hair that already exists. It should not be painted onto the skin but onto the hair. If your brows are bare apply the pencil very, very lightly. The feelings about painted-on brows are universally negative. The color should be only a shade darker than the hair on your head.

Blush:

The biggest problem with using blush is the choice of color. Try to think of it logically and you will understand. No person I have ever seen or heard of naturally blushes orange or anything close to it. Blush is to simulate your natural color, to give the skin a healthy look. It is not supposed to show off your blouse. Its purpose is to show off you. Any blush with yellow in it or brick, peach, coral etc., demands attention and will always be seen. If you want an arty or off-beat look makeup is not the best way to do it. If you want to show off your attributes, look natural. Do not use blush to draw attention to your makeup.

Find a blush color with pink in it. This may mean burgundy for darker skins and mauve for lighter ones. The best way is to have no makeup on, pinch your skin and see what color your cheeks are turning. That is the color of blush you should buy. Another way is to look at the pink at the tips of your fingers when you squeeze them and buy a blush that shade or a touch lighter. Most cosmetic companies use yellows in their blushes. Be selective in choosing colors.

Lips:

This is the part of your makeup that changes with personality and color preference. You can wear any color of lipstick if the rest of your makeup is right. Any color works on the lips if you like it. If you wear lipstick to match your outfit you will have more of a forties look. For the most natural look your lip color should be nearly equal to the intensity of your eye color. Light pinks tend to have a young outdoors look. Rose colors are the best natural business look. Brights add pizzazz and sexiness. Dark colors (in relation to your eyes) are mysterious and sensuous. Corals and oranges are arty and off-beat looking.

Lining the lips in a dark color is for the stage, not the real world. Painting beyond your natural lip lines does not make your lips look larger and it is unbecoming. You may not like your thin lips but this technique only works with a camera and very good lighting.

Coverstick:

This is a flesh colored stick (it looks like lipstick) to be applied under your foundation and should not be a yellow tone. It is best if your coverstick is darker than your foundation.

Mascara:

The brush is the most important item of the mascara tube. You want a brush that doesn't clump the eyelashes together. Bacteria develop easily in mascara and a fresh tube should be purchased about every six weeks at the least.

Brushes:

A sable brush is worth every penny. It blends makeup well for a more natural look. Wash your brushes often in warm water and a little soap. Sponge applicators, your fingers and synthetic brushes are hard on your complexion, don't do as nice a job, and—except for the fingers—don't last as long. The lack of a good brush is one of the main reasons for poor makeup application.

BASIC APPLICATION OF MAKEUP

Now that the slate is as clean as we can get it, let's learn how easy makeup is. The only changes you will want to make in the method I am about to give you will be explained when you get to your style.

1. Clean your face.

2. Moisturize your face and let the moisturizer soak into your skin.

3. With a coverstick, run over any red blotchy areas or marks on your skin. Do not blend yet.

4. Apply your foundation and blend lightly over the cover stick as you go. Put foundation on the eyelids. This helps eye shadows last and keeps skin even.

5. With a large full brush apply your blush. Look in the mirror and smile. Do you see the apple of your cheek? It's the place that aunts pinch when you're a child. Put your blush on this spot and blend it by brushing back and up on your cheek. I can't stress strongly enough not to blush in a pie or wedge shape. The blush that goes past your cheek is only residue left on the brush. When you go out in the cold, how do you blush? With few exceptions we blush at the cheek and nose.

6. Apply gray or brown shadow in and just above the crease of the eyelid, creating an "arch." Use an angled eye shadow brush. Apply the shadow much darker than you think you should; it will be blended later. Then fill in all the space between the line you created and your eyelash. The outside of the arch can be finished in one of two ways. If your eye turns down at the outside then brush a line up to the brow. Any other shape of eye should simply complete the arch. (See illustrations 21 and 22.) You may feel ridiculous but your shadow can't be too dark at this point. It will be blended.

Illustration #21: Create an arch by putting shadow in the crease of the lid and just above. With the same shadow fill in the space from the arch down to the eyelash. (For more instruction see page 114.)

Illustration #22: If you have eyes that turn down at the corners finish the outside of the "arch" by lifting the color to the eyebrow. (For more instruction see page 114.)

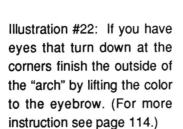

Using either a face powder, a skin-colored shadow or a very light pink shadow (fair people only), brush from the arch to the eyebrow, then brush over all of the eye shadow already applied. Continue to blend until all hard lines of makeup are gone. Draw an imaginary line from the outside tip of your eye up to the outside tip of your eyebrow; no makeup should be outside that line. Reapply on any areas that were blended too much. Blend all shadows again.

7. Using a gray or brown for light-colored eyes and brown, black or navy for dark-colored eyes, apply your liner on the bottom lid only. Start at the outside edge of the eye and go inward. This line can continue in to the center of the eye if done softly. It is also very attractive to put only a very short but bolder line on the outside one-eighth or one-quarter of the eye. If your eye tends to turn down at the corner go out as far as you can without leaving the eye itself.

8. Always apply your mascara to the bottom lashes first and only on the tips. On the top lash start at the base and roll the brush in your fingers as you move upward. If the lashes clump or you can't separate them you have too much on or the mascara is too heavy. Even if you have always worn black, give dark brown a try. Dark brown has a more natural look and is better for work.

9. Apply a moisturizer if lips are chapped or dry. With your finger rub some lip color into the center of the lip to stain it. This helps it to maintain some color over the course of the day. Then with a lipstick or a brush, apply your color within the natural lines of your lips. If your lips are all you see when you look in the mirror the effect is too bright or dark for your eyes. In this case use your same eye makeup and darken the eyes for more glamour or drama. For a professional or natural look, lighten the lip color.

10. Apply a soft coat of face powder with a large sable brush. Be sure you go over the eyelids. This will blend and stabilize your makeup.

To look terrific and show off your skin and eyes you never need to know anything else about makeup than what you've learned here.

A more casual way to apply makeup:

1. Cleanse and moisturize.
2. Apply face powder or foundation.
3. Apply blush to cheeks, nose, forehead and chin. (If it's too bright your blush is wrong).
4. Mascara.
5. Lip gloss.

A more glamourous look in your makeup:

1. Wear brighter or darker lipstick.
2. Apply shadows and liner even darker. Odd colors, shiny shadows, thicker or longer eye liner are not the way to add glamour. Try using the other elements of style to add emphasis.

A few suggestions for those who want to experiment with eye color:

Green eyes: Replace crease and lid eye shadow color with purple, or add a thin line of purple shadow to lid above lashes.

Brown eyes: Replace crease and lid eye shadow color with teal or add a thin line of teal shadow to lid above lashes.

Blue eyes: Wear brown shadow a little darker than daytime wear.

Hazel or neutral eyes: Select color you want to bring out and wear the makeup suggested above for that color.

CHOOSING YOUR FAVORITE MAKEUP

If you looked just as good in each of the following, which would you most love to wear? Makeup that is:

- As soft as possible, showing off the skin. (7)
- Glossy, vibrant and colorful. (9)
- No makeup at all. (1)
- Mascara and blush but with no foundation. (2)
- Understated, neat, and precise looking. (3)
- Elegant, with accent on the eyes. (4)
- Very dramatic. (5)
- Fresh and pretty. (8)
- From none to tons depending on my mood. (6)

Make your choice and then write the corresponding number in the box provided on page 139.

The Element Of Hair

It is so easy to look in a magazine and love the hair styles on the models. It seems our hair is always too thick, thin, curly, straight, blonde or red for whatever we want to have done with it. It is frustrating to get a bad hair style. It is, however, not entirely the fault of the stylist.

When you sit down in the chair and you're asked what you want, either be precise with the hairdresser or you're liable to get the wrong effect. If you're not asked what you want be sure and bring it up. You don't need to know the exact hair style, but you do need to give the stylist some guidelines.

Hairstylists, like the members of the fashion industry, promote trendy styles and believe hair should be as wild or original as it can be. This may be true for the entertainment industry, but not in the world you and I live in. A good stylist knows her job is to listen to what you want and to use her expertise to help you get it. Your hairdresser should be able to tell you what your hair will and won't do. She should be able to give you a variety of ideas that would be good for your face. I also feel strongly that she should tell you the pros and cons of any chemicals she uses and how to keep your hair healthy looking.

Beyond expecting your hairdresser to be a mind reader, there are a few other reasons women are often unhappy with their hair.

A lot of women compromise style while hair is growing out. This is not necessary and in fact may discourage you from growing your hair longer. Let your hairdresser know what your ultimate goal is. Also let her know that regardless of the time it takes you want good styles along the way. Do yourself and your self esteem a favor and don't just stop going to get your hair cut because you want to wear it long. It may take longer to grow, but you'll look better along the way and it can be fun because you will experience a variety of looks as your hair grows.

Your hair is not a place to scrimp in order to stay in your budget. I hear too many women say, "I can't afford to go to someone like that." You will always find the extra $20 for the things that are important to you. You can not ignore your hair when you look in the mirror. It is the most dominant "accessory" you have that shows off your skin, eyes and the features of your face. It speaks eloquently *(nonverbally)* about your health, hygiene, self esteem and even your competence. Please, know that you are worth it. Save money some other place on some other item of your budget that doesn't have such an effect on your beauty and self acceptance.

Everyone needs a hair professional, and it is important to find a stylist with whom you can work, so that between the two of you an attractive and appropriate style can be found. If your stylist keeps suggesting a new style and you want to stick with your old one at least talk about it. Ask her why she thinks you need a change. Have another hairdresser in the salon come over and offer her opinion on your hair style. Be sure your guidelines are voiced and then give the professional a chance. They really can do wonders if you just communicate with them.

Selecting A Hairstylist

Some hairdressers have more talent to give you what you want than others. To find a stylist that you will be happy with, find one that:
- ••Actively listens to you.
- ••Has a personality you relate to.
- ••Presents herself in a manner you admire.
- ••Has been recommended by someone whose hair you like.
- ••Likes to get ideas from pictures you bring in.
- ••Continues to attend classes to improve her skills.
- ••Gives you more than just adjectives (cute, beautiful, smashing etc.) to explain why you should or shouldn't have a certain style.
- ••Has a hair style that in your opinion is good on her.
- ••Can give you several suggestions within your guidelines.
- ••Teaches you how to fix your hair style by yourself.

If you follow these suggestions, you'll get a stylist who will better serve you and your needs. Just because you have not addressed hair professionals in this manner before does not make it inappropriate. You pay for the service; it might as well be the service you want.

Guidelines For a Flattering Hair Style

Many women rely on facial shape charts to decide what style they should wear. There is no need to make it complicated; just give the stylist these guidelines:

Three points on your face to consider:
1. The brow.
2. The cheekbone.
3. The jaw. (See illustration 23.)

Three points of your hair to consider:
1. Top of your head.
2. Sides above the ears.
3. Sides below the ears. (See illustrations 24, 25.)

To best show off your eyes and face you want the cheekbone to appear to be wider than the other two points on your face. If your cheeks are the widest you can wear any style you prefer and still flatter your face.

If it is your jaw that is widest or you wish to trim the lower face you will want a hair style that has volume on the top. The sides above the ears should have the next volume and the least should be below the ears. (See illustration 24.)

For example a short hair cut should be longer or permed on top so that you add height. Short on the sides is fine because there is no hair below the ears. A shoulder length style needs to be moussed or layered for fullness at the temples. Regardless of your preferred style, just keep in mind these proportions.

If it is your brow that is widest or you wish to broaden your jaw line you will want a hair style with most of the volume of hair below the ears, secondly at the sides above the ears and not much volume on top. A page boy with bangs would work or a wedge that is full at the jaw line. (See illustration 25.)

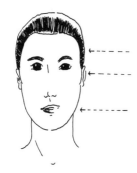

Illustration #23: The three points of the face:

Brow

Cheekbone

Jaw

The eyes and face are most flattered when the cheekbones look like they are the widest of the three points.

Hair style is the best way to flatter the face. Consider the volume of hair at each of the three points.

Illustration #24: If you wish to thin the lower jaw and neck, then the volume in your haircut should be greatest on top. The sides above the ears should be next in volume of hair.

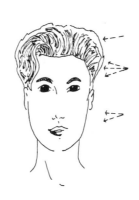

Illustration #25: If you want to broaden or strengthen the jawline then the hair below the ears should have the most volume. The top of the head should have the least volume.

Many styles fit these guidelines. These are just examples.

• Bangs worn straight across the forehead strengthen and square the jaw and shorten the face.

• Hair styles with height on top lengthen and trim the face.

• Hair styles that are full just below the ears, such as some wedges, lengthen the neck.

• Long hair hanging straight down the sides of the face draws attention away from the eyes and makes the nose appear larger.

• Shoulder length hair with a lot of volume at the temples will diminish roundness.

• Asymmetrical lines are more flattering to any face, such as parts on the side instead of the middle, or bangs pulled back on one side.

Don't be shy about giving direction to your hair stylist. She will appreciate the opinions you express about you preferences because they will reflect your interest in making yourself more attractive. That is her job and any information she can get from you to improve how she can make you look will be to her benefit, and certainly to yours. Once you start working with your stylist in this fashion you'll be on the road to hair styles you like.

CHOOSING YOUR FAVORITE HAIR STYLE

Select your favorite hair style from the ones below. If your hair could do it, which of the following would you love to wear?

- Short, wash-and-wear haircut. (1)
- Hair slicked back or worn asymmetrically. (5)
- Uncontrolled hair, possibly frizzy. (6)
- Long soft and flowing hair, with a gentle curl. (7)
- Healthy, bouncy fresh-looking style. (2)
- Short at neck with longer hair on top, softly curled or long hair pulled up in a soft roll on top. (4)
- Shoulder length blunt cut, straight or with very little curl. (3)
- Long and full hair worn toward the face, with a lot of layers. (9)
- Curly around the face; able to wear it with a variety of hair accessories. (8)

Make your choice and then write the corresponding number in the box provided on page139.

What's Wrong With This Picture?

Illustration #26

Using your knowledge of the Elements of Style see if you can tell what is wrong with this picture. Assume that this woman likes to be feminine and comfortable at the same time and that she prefers a casual, professional look. The errors of dress are:

1. The cardigan is too short. This adds weight to the hips and stomach and shortens the waist, imparting a "frumpy" look.

2. The skirt is the wrong length. A full skirt that touches the middle of the calf adds weight to the legs and hips. It gives the wearer a round, dowdy and shorter look.

3. The cardigan is pulled across the chest. This makes the bust look larger, the upper body squarer and heavier.

4. The nylons are not the same tone as the skirt. This has the effect of shortening the whole body and adds weight to the legs and hips. It also makes the clothes look of poorer quality.

5. The sleeves are worn long. This length adds to the roundness of the body and shortens the waist.

6. The blouse is tight at the ribs causing the front to pull to the side.

7. The earrings are too small. As a result they don't show off the eyes.

How To Improve The Look!

Illustration #27

By making a few adjustments, the appearance of the model in illustration #26 can be greatly improved. As you can see, here in illustration 27, the changes necessary to stay in style and to flatter the body do not require a lot of money. Here are the changes:

1. Lengthen the cardigan.
2. Lengthen the full skirt.
3. The two edges of the cardigan fall straight down across the breasts.
4. The nylons are the same tone as the skirt to give more height and a more finished look. Knee-high hose would be optional.
5. Sleeves worn at three-quarters length thin the lower body and lengthen the upper body.
6. Choosing one larger size of blouse is not only more comfortable and flattering, but it allows the wearer to look good if she decides to remove the cardigan.
7. Larger earrings compliment the eyes and face.
8. Hair with most of its volume on the top of the head slims the face. A soft curl makes the face more feminine.

What's Wrong With This Picture?

Illustration #28

Using your knowledge of the Elements of Style see if you can discover what's wrong with this picture. Assume that the woman in this picture likes a casual, simple, sporty look. The errors of dress are:

1. A snug fitting blouse without shoulder pads makes the hips look larger and it gives the impression of lower quality.

2. The closed collar makes the square jaw look even squarer.

3. More volume in the hair below the ears than above has the effect of lengthening and squaring the face.

4. The lack of accessories creates an unfinished look.

5. Long sleeves give a slumped-shoulder, gangly look even though the model is broad shouldered.

6. Pants are too tight at the hips.

7. Pants are a little short, adding weight to the hips and thighs.

8. Shoes that are darker than the pants further shorten the torso, adding weight to the lower body.

How To Improve The Look!

Illustration #29

For a sporty look that is more flattering you don't have to "dress up." The changes are simple:

1. A looser fit in a blouse with shoulder pads and with sleeves pushed to three-quarters length creates an overall body proportion in which hips and chest look approximately equal. Also, the waist achieves a trimmer look.

2. Longer length pants fitting loosely at the hips slim the lower body and gives the whole torso a better shape.

3. Opening up the collar creates a neckline that is higher in the back and lower in the front. This softens the face, lengthens and trims the neck.

4. Hair less square on top with none below the ears, helps to flatter the eyes and face as well as give a more feminine look.

5. Shoes the same tone as the pants help lengthen and trim the leg.

6. Accessories add a more finished and attractive look to the model without losing the feeling of casualness.

What's Wrong With This Picture?

Illustration #30

Using your knowledge of the Elements of Style see if you can discover what is wrong with this picture. Assume the woman in the picture wants a professional look and loves accessories.

1. Too many accessories give a junky and "tacky" look. This creates confusion in the outfit and draws attention away from the wearer.

2. A jacket without shoulder pads or ones that are too small shortens the upper body and adds weight to the lower body.

3. Long unruly hair is inconsistent with a suit for work. The hair shown also has too much volume below the ears for the full cheeks of the model.

4. A collar that has a horizontal line across the neck lends a masculine and square look to the face.

5. The skirt is too tight at the hips. This not only creates the illusion of weight, it has the effect of cheapening the quality of the clothes.

6. The A-line skirt is in the wrong length. Mid-calf skirts are not flattering to the legs or hips, or overall body.

7. Dark hose with a light skirt shortens the whole body creating a heavier, less sleek, less finished look.

How To Improve The Look!

Illustration #31

For a more professional and flattering look still using fun accessories, the following changes are suggested.

1. Put one large accessory near the face (a pin is used in this picture). All other accessories are smaller.

2. The jacket has a soft shoulder pad and is now longer. This jacket flatters the whole body and looks of higher quality.

3. The skirt is straight and is brought up to a classic length. This professionalizes the outfit, trims the body, and adds style.

4. The high neckline is looser so that it drapes down in the front softening the face and cheek.

5. The hair is pulled back for a cleaner, less busy, more professional look.

6. The hose match the skirt, finishing and adding a quality look to the outfit.

3

THE INDIVIDUAL STYLES

How to use the Personality Profiles and Elements of each style to select and project the image you want.

Δ Δ Δ Δ

Selecting your individual style is intriguing, enjoyable and probably one of the main reasons you chose to read this book. Some women have one core style. They may adopt a few elements of another style for a special occasion, but they have one core style that best fits their personality. Some women have a combination of two styles. This means they are a combination of the characteristics of both styles.

There are several ways to decide upon your style. To determine yours, do the following:

1. Turn to the Elements of Style Tally Sheet on page 139. If any number appears five or more times, consider that your core style.

2. If no number appears five or more time, you will need to read the profiles of each of the style numbers that appear most often. Select the style that best describes your personality and consider that to be your core style.

3. If you still cannot decide between two styles, your style is probably a combination of the two. Actually over 50 percent of the women in the U.S. have combination styles. To create a successful combination style, you need to look at the elements of each style being considered. For each element, select your favorite of the two styles. For example, if you are a combination of style #2 and #7, turn to the element of proportion for each style and decide which best fits you. Then do the same with colors, prints, fabrics, etc. Be sure to make a decision for each element.

After you have decided upon your style, read through the elements and then turn to "Time To Take Action" on page 247. This section will help you clean out your closet and prioritize your purchases.

Besides learning how to dress to project your personality, there are other ways to use the information about the styles:

1. Read the profiles of other styles to help you better understand the people in your life.

2. Use the elements of other styles to project different sides of your personality. This can be used for special occasions, job interviews, 'hot' dates or simply to express a mood you're in. By using elements of a different style, you will prevent the expensive mistake of buying something you wear only once and that does not fit the rest of your wardrobe.

3. Use the profiles and elements to project the characteristics and personality that you would like to become. This can be successful in business or in personal relationships. For example, you may feel that by projecting

the characteristics of style #3, you will be taken more seriously at work. Using a couple of the elements from style #3 will allow you to do this without costing a lot of money or causing confusion. At the same time, you'll get to keep your individuality.

You may not like everything in your style's elements. Don't give up. It may be that you have not seen a color, fabric, proportion, etc. with other elements of your style. For example, you may have had a bad experience with long skirts in the past because you wore them with the wrong jackets, etc. Maybe you have disliked brown because you wore it with other colors which are not in your style. All I suggest is that you not give up until you do some experimentation.

Finally, remember that there are not better or worse styles, just different ones. There are no bad or good traits in any personality, since that is all a matter of opinion. The only mistake you can make in selecting your style is to not select your favorite. The opinion that matters is your own. Do you see and accept the good and wonder of you? That means acceptance rather than criticism of the sides to you that you want to work on. Honestly, I have never met a woman who can't look beautiful. By learning to present the beauty inside of you, you'll have better self esteem, be more accepted for who you are, be more content and you will be more beautiful. The most beautiful women in the world are those who accept themselves and reflect their assets.

Elements Of Style Tally Sheet

As you make your choice at the end of each section place the results here.

Proportion	A.	_____	(from page 84)
	B.	_____	(from page 85)
	C.	_____	(from page 86)
Color		_____	(from page 89)
Prints		_____	(from page 91)
Fabrics		_____	(from page 94)
Accessories		_____	(from page 109)
Makeup		_____	(from page 122)
Hair		_____	(from page 129)

Most Common number above   _____

Second (if three or more)   _____

Third (if three or more)   _____

Each number represents one of the nine individual styles. If any number appears five or more times consider it your core style. For further explanation see page 136.

STYLE #1 -THE STRAIGHT SHOOTER

Personality Profile

If you choose to dress in this style these are the traits you project:

Hard-working
Reliable
Honest
Practical
Safe
Dependable
Easy to be with
Good at laughing at yourself
Love animals
Conservative
Grounded
Trustworthy
Principled
Neighborly
Humble
House is comfortable and others feel at home there
Down to earth
Traditional
Solid
Informal
Competent
Honorable
Sincere
Find it hard to compliment self
Do for others often at your own expense

If you have the personality characteristics described in this profile you are the "Straight Shooter." You are truly what you present yourself to be. You don't have mystery or wear a mask. You are predictable and stable in your morals and attitudes. You are the salt-of-the-earth type of person. Reliability, honesty, practicality and conservatism are at the heart of everything you do. You enjoy the country, hiking, outdoors, gardening, watching sports, and informal environments. You are comfortable to be around and prefer a more informal and relaxed life. You are a hard-working person who will roll up your sleeves for a job that needs doing, and enjoy camaraderie and laughter.

The unpretentious and natural attitude of your style is refreshing and balancing to many. As a friend there are few to compare to you in loyalty. The Straight Shooter is usually loved by animals and visa versa. As a partner, the Straight Shooter is dependable and is comfortable with traditional roles in marriage. You are a woman who will do the "right" thing for your family. As a parent you will be a teacher of children and show them the importance of honesty and work.

As a Straight Shooter when you lack self confidence it usually shows up as self neglect. It is common for your style to sacrifice your health and attractiveness with the excuse of not having enough time. There is always time for what is important but when you don't feel good about yourself taking care of *you* becomes a low priority. There are a lot of Straight Shooters who don't feel they are worth the nice hair cut, the massage, or the skin care products. I often hear things like, "There are so many things I have to get my kids or husband first." In times of low self esteem, the Straight Shooter may be too conservative, too safe and not take enough time for fun. As a Straight Shooter you should try to understand that putting other people before yourself to the detriment of your own health, peace, and happiness is not appreciated or respected. Taking time for yourself is the best gift you can give to those who care for you. If you give it a try you will be surprised. Never be shy about your femininity and personal attractiveness.

The Straight Shooter often has a home that is slightly rumpled and lived in. As a hostess she is one who makes people feel at home quickly. I often give the example of the Straight Shooter who serves guests the first beverage when they arrive and then shows them the refrigerator, suggesting that they help themselves. I usually find blues or earth tones in the home of a Straight Shooter, and many times a rustic or very casual decor.

The nonverbal skills that will be helpful to you as a Straight Shooter in relationship building are eye contact, smiling and active listening. These will reinforce the honesty of who you are or want to be. If you are giving up too much of yourself for the sake of others, your body language, health, hygiene and tone of voice will be affected.

Your clothes should be comfortable and easy to care for. Cleanliness is the essence of your beauty. You are probably underdressed for some occasions, find weekend wear a breeze, evening wear the most frustrating. In fact, you probably see putting together any kind of an outfit more of a hassle than fun. Believe me you can be comfortable and look great too.

Although you want to look good, you want to do it without fuss and in as short a time as possible. Your style has too many other things to do to consider dressing a priority. For your self esteem I suggest two things. First, schedule time for working out, haircuts, quiet time etc. You

You should put yourself in a higher priority. Everyone in your life will benefit from the energy this releases. Second, money spent on good skin care and some basic quality pieces of clothing is priceless to your self esteem. You probably dislike shopping. But if you follow the elements of your style as shown immediately following this profile you will cut wasted time and money significantly. The element most often ignored by your style of woman is proportion. You should make it a top priority to clean out your closet of any jackets or skirts in the wrong lengths. You shouldn't waste time and money on alterations of clothes that are showing wear. You should tell the outfit goodbye and thank you. Accessories are often neglected too. This is usually because you have not viewed them as the practical and money saving element they are. Nothing will bring more value to your purchases than accessories and proportion. If you do nothing else, you should do yourself a favor and start here.

The work environment that allows you to shine the best with your own qualities is one where you are not asked to compromise your ethics. You are adaptable and can be relied upon to get the job done. The work ethics in the business world often coincide with yours. A job that offers opportunity for self responsibility and appreciation for a job well done is right up your alley. If you can find an informal, hard-working environment with a clear cut job description you will have less stress at work. A work place that requires communication will work best for you if there are other Straight Shooters in the group. A highly creative environment will bring you frustration unless you can accept an attitude that values promptness with work assignments less than you do.

Remember it takes all kinds to make this world the colorful and worthwhile place it is. No personality is better, only different. Instead of wishing you were more like someone else, pat yourself on the back. You possess some of the most admired traits in our society. By the way, the most important woman of my life has a lot of the Straight Shooter style, my mom. I can't tell you how often over the years my brothers and I wished she would take more time for herself and how great it is to see her do so more and more. I know the people who love you feel the same way. Give it a try, you'll be amazed by the results.

Style #1 - The Straight Shooter

Illustration #32A   Illustration #32B   Illustration #32C

Illustration #32A

Dress: Lavender, cotton knit.
Necklace: Navy beads.
Belt: Navy, leather with silver buckle.
Earrings: Silver.
Hose: Light gray.
Shoes: Taupe.

Illustration #32B

Blouse: True blue, cotton broadcloth.
Pants: Taupe.
Cardigan: Taupe and true blue.
Earrings: Gold and blue.
Belt: Brown.
Shoes: Taupe.

Illustration #32C

Jacket: Navy blue, wool flannel with silver buttons.
Blouse: White, washable silk.
Skirt: Medium gray with navy, tweed.
Earrings: Red and silver.
Pocket scarf: Red.
Necklace: Silver.
Shoe: Navy two-tone.

Elements Of The Straight Shooter's Style

<u>Proportion</u>

<u>Skirt Lengths/Styles</u>: Classic length
                              Straight
                              Soft pleat
                              Gathered
                              Wide pleat
                  Long length
                              Dirndl
                              Straight
                              Trouser style

Be sure the waistbands are comfortable when you sit down.

<u>Jacket Lengths</u>: Long—just below rear
Long—finger tip

<u>Style of Jackets or
            Cardigans:</u> Notch lapel
Narrow shawl lapel
Double-breasted
Deep "V"
Breast pocket
Gold or silver buttons

<u>Necklines</u>: Oxford collar
Turtle necks
Mock turtles
Notch collars

Sleeves:	Long, pushed to three-quarter length
	Elbow-length
	Three-quarter

Colors

Core	Accent
Navy	White
Brown	Soft pink
Beige	Lemon yellow
Camel	Jade green
Medium gray	Blue red
	Aqua
	True blue
	Baby blue
	Lavender

Any blues make great accent colors. Core colors are basic and practical.

Prints

Subtle geometric
Glen plaids
Tartan plaids
Checks
Stripes

Fabrics

Cotton	Cable knit
Popcorn knit	Heavy cotton knit
Wool gabardine	Wool flannel

Fine wale corduroy	Camel hair
Cotton flannel tweeds	Washable silk
Taffeta seersucker	Velveteen
Tweeds	Oxford cotton

It is important that fabrics feel comfortable on your body. Blouses and casual wear should be washable. Blends of fabrics are fine and synthetics often add to the life of a garment.

Makeup

See makeup application section. Try the casual option (page 121) first if you are more comfortable with it. Progress to the Basic (page 118) application as you increase in confidence.

Lip colors: Clear
                Light pinks

Hair

Easy care
Short
Casual

A little highlighting or curl on top is a good idea. For examples see illustrations 32 A, B, and C.

Accessory Wardrobe

"Basic" refers to gold, silver, and pearl.

Necklaces: Chains 24 to 30 inch long at least 1/8 inch
thick
        1 Each basic
        1 Each in two accent colors

Earrings: Nickle to quarter size
        2 Each basic
        1 Each of two accent colors

Bracelets: Chain-like at least 1/8 inch thick
        1 Gold
        1 Silver

Pins: Larger than a silver dollar
        1 Each basic

Belts: 1 Inch thick, no buckles, cloth or leather
        1 Cream or white
        1 Navy
        1 For each jacket color in wardrobe

Shoes: Pumps
        1 Pair navy
        1 Pair taupe or gray
    Flats
        1 Pair navy
        1 Pair taupe or gray

Purses:	A lot of pockets made of a practical and long lasting material
	1 with navy
	1 with taupe or gray

Nylons:	Charcoal gray
	Silver gray

Detachable Shoulder Pads

Sleevebands

When selecting the way you want to accessorize an outfit, use the suggestions on page 107. The suggestions best for your style use two finishing accessories (for casual), or three finishing accessories (for office or evening).

STYLE #2 - THE ALL AMERICAN

Personality Profile

If you choose to dress in this style these are the traits you project:

Energetic with an up and at 'em attitude
Natural
Love comfort and minimum care
Feel health is the essence of beauty
Sporty and love the outdoors
Tomboy as a child
Fast moving
High spirited
Team player
Curious
Quick-witted
Accept other's differences
Fun to be with
Vigorous
Spunky
Playful
Lively
Mischievous
Peppery
Alert
Snappy
Laughing
Girl next door
Active or Athletic
Impatient
Shy of revealing the role of femininity in your life

If you have the personality characteristics described in this profile you are called an All American. You are a high-spirited woman who was a tomboy in your childhood, the girl next door who played sports with the boys instead of games with girls. You are a woman who loves physical activity, is spunky and fun loving. You also can stand on your own against adversity but seem to do it in a positive way. You don't have to be the center of attention, but often are simply because of your enthusiasm for life. Lively and mischievous, you are a woman who isn't overly serious. You work well, but have fun while accomplishing the task at hand. Although often patient with kids or animals, yours is a "let's get going," "let's get it done" attitude.

Your energetic and positive attitude is a natural draw to people today. You probably have great buddy-like relationships with men. Because you are a little shy about your feminine role you may find romance difficult to slip into. The Straight Shooter may have a well-trained dog, but you probably have an animal that is physically active and rambunctious. As a partner or friend you are a supporter and will do physical work and play right beside the men. As a parent, you like to teach sportsmanship and self challenge. Because you set the example of getting through tough times with a smile, your style of woman is a wonderful parent for developing a good attitude in children.

As an All American when you lack self confidence it is usually demonstrated as hyperactivity. Often your type of woman doesn't take time to listen to others. You should slow down your talking, avoid interrupting and work on holding still in order to develop respect from others. Learning to relax through meditation, regular work-outs or reading can make it easier for you to direct your energy.

Most All Americans win in our society because of the universal admiration for enthusiasm. The only thing that will hold you back is thinking that communication means talking. You are excellent at getting people pumped up and can use your enthusiasm to make work and home the fun places you want. If you overuse this talent you will tire out many people. You may think that jiggling or bouncing your leg is just a way to release energy, but it makes many people nervous and they are likely to see you as unsettled.

Your home probably has a little of the country feeling to it. You love a lot of natural light and primary and clear colors are wonderful for your decor. You are not a sit-at-home and watch television type of person. You may have projects going on in the yard or in the house most of the time. If not, you are probably busy with community involvement and family or club activities.

The nonverbal skills of the All American that will be helpful in relationships are active listening, body language, controlling facial expressions and the tone of voice. These will help her gain respect for her ability in dealing with people. The difference between an All American person who becomes a leader versus one who stays in a less desirable position is usually found in the strength of her listening skills.

In your choice of clothing it is important for you to have a fresh and youthful look. It is equally important to be comfortable. This can be done without jeopardizing professionalism at work. Health is the essence of your beauty, so you should make it a top priority to develop a lifestyle that promotes it. You will notice immediate, positive results from this decision simply because you will be more true to yourself. Because you are active, you probably have a decent figure and tend to buy clothes that fit and are comfortable regardless of how they match with the rest of your closet. You enjoy shopping for work-out clothes, sweats, jeans and other casual and active wear. This is great, but these garments are not appropriate for most work places.

When fashion coincides with your style, you may tend to wear the fad for occasions that are not quite appropriate. Recent examples of this are the mini-skirt or stirrups with the long sweater worn without nylons and flat shoes. This is a great look but it may not be applicable for the work place.

A pony tail or hair past your shoulders would be most appropriate worn up or back in another fashion if you want to be respected in the business world. You can have a fresh, enthusiastic, and young look and still be comfortable, respected and yourself. You don't need to buy entire outfits and wear them only the way they are purchased. This will cost you more money and time than you need to spend. If you understand and make use of accessories, you will find shopping for and wearing clothes a lot more worthwhile and fun.

To project a listening attitude it will behoove the All American to adopt a few elements from the Gentlewoman. Also, the Straight Shooter can give the All American style a reliable and down to earth projection.

The work environment that allows you to best express your personality is one that promotes teamwork. If you find your associates are downers or tend to have a negative attitude, it will wear on you in time. Even though you may have a positive outlook you will be much happier if you have at least a few people around you with laughter to share. You have a knack for getting people to see the lighter side of life. This gift can work wonders in a high-stress work situation. A social, reliable, and hard-working work world is a place where you shine. The communication work environment is best for you. If your work involves corporate people it will become more important for you to learn to listen and to develop composure. If your work is creative it will be to your advantage to make clear your work ethics and expectations. Highly creative people are notorious for forgetting or letting time and deadlines slip away.

The enthusiasm you are blessed with is contagious. This is such a positive trait and so loved in our culture that it will serve you well. Your enthusiasm will always give you a young attitude. This is fine as long as it isn't consistently out of control or silly. By the way, many times my All American clients have laughingly said things like, "I'm not impatient, I simply like things done yesterday, or sooner." All American clients who have made an effort to pay constant attention to listening skills have reported that it pays off immeasurably. This effort on your part will provide you with more appreciation and understanding by others, but don't let anybody curtail your enthusiasm. It's who you are.

Style #2 - The All American

Illustration #33A   Illustration #33B   Illustration #33C

Illustration #33A

Jacket: Cobalt, with jade green, hot pink and turquoise plaid, wool-rayon blend.
Turtleneck: White, cotton knit.
Skirt: Cobalt, wool gabardine.
Necklace: Gold.
Earrings: Gold and hot pink.
Belt: Hot pink.
Hose: Gray.
Shoes: Navy.

Illustration #33B

Jacket and walking short: Navy, raw silk.
Shirt: White and red stripe, light-weight cotton blend.
Hair band: Red.
Earrings: Red.
Belt: Red.
Hose: Cream.
Shoes: Navy.

Illustration #33C

Dress: Taupe, brushed cotton with purple denim epaulets, cuffs and belt.
Earrings: Purple.
Hose: Gray.
Shoes: Taupe.

Elements Of The All American's Style

<u>Proportion</u>

<u>Skirt Lengths/Style</u>: Classic length
                                      Straight
                    Mini length
                        Stitch-down pleat
                        Straight
                        Gore
                    Long length
                        Stitch-down pleat
                        Straight
                        Gore
                        Wide pleat

<u>Jacket Length</u>: Waist length (with full pant only)
Long—just below rear
Long—finger tip

<u>Style of Jackets or</u>
      <u>Cardigans</u>: Notch lapel
Wide shawl lapel
1 Button front
Boyfriend style
Prints
Bomber style

<u>Necklines:</u> Cowl neck
"V" neck
Turtle
Boat neck

Shirt neck

Sleeves: Long pushed to three-quarter length
                     Sleeveless
                     Elbow length

Colors

Core	Accent
Taupe	Hot pink
Khaki	True red
Dark navy	True blue
Purple	Light pink
White	White
	Sunshine yellow
	Turquoise
	Cobalt blue
	Orange
	Green

Primary colors are excellent accent colors. Give yellow a try as an accent; you'll be surprised.

Prints

Checks
Any plaid that you like
White background prints
Small dots
Colorful tweeds

Mixed blue, green, pinks and purples all of the same depth of color are excellent.

Fabrics

Light weight silk	All sweater knits
Cotton flannel	Raw silk
Cotton broadcloth	Cotton knit
Cotton blends	Brushed cotton
Wool gabardine	Denim
Crisp feeling synthetic blends	

Crisp and linear look. Smooth-textured and comfortable fabrics are best. Raw silk is an excellent mix and match suit fabric.

Makeup

See makeup application section. Try the casual option for weekends (page 121). The glamour suggestions are still natural enough for this style. The basic application works well for both work and evening (page 118).

Lip Colors: Pinks
            Roses

Hair

Bouncy
Fresh
Healthy
Out of your face

A younger style looks okay if you wash and wear it. Highlights are good. For examples see illustrations 33A, B and C.

Accessory Wardrobe

"Basic" refers to gold and silver.

Necklaces: Chains 14 to 30 inches long at least 1/4 inch
            thick
                1 Each basic
                1 Core color
                1 Accent color

Earrings: Nickle to quarter size
                1 Each basic
                1 Core color
                1 Accent color with gold or silver
            Dangle or hoop
                1 Each basic

Bracelets: Band, simple at least 1/4 inch thick
                1 Each basic
                1 Gold/silver combination

Pins: Silver dollar size or larger
                1 Each basic
                1 Silver/gold

Belts: 1/2 inch wide, no buckle or small buckle
                1 Navy
                1 Cream
                1 Core color
                1 Accent color
                1 For each jacket or cardigan color

Shoes:	Pumps
	1 Pair navy
	1 Pair taupe or khaki
	Flats
	1 Pair navy
	1 Pair taupe or khaki
	1 Pair accent color

Shoes: Pumps
　　　1 Pair navy
　　　1 Pair taupe or khaki
　　Flats
　　　1 Pair navy
　　　1 Pair taupe or khaki
　　　1 Pair accent color

Purses: Very small with shoulder strap
　　　1 With navy or brown
　　　1 With taupe or khaki
　　　1 Fanny pack in leather

Nylons: Charcoal
　　Grey
　　Cream (can use with navy skirts and
　　　　shoes if blouse or upper half of
　　　　garment is white or of a light color).

Detachable shoulder pads

Sleevebands

When selecting the way you want to accessorize an outfit, use the suggestions on page 107. The suggestions best for your style use two finishing accessories (for casual), three finishing accessories (for evening and office), or one large finishing accessory (for casual or evening).

STYLE #3 - THE ACHIEVER

Personality Profile

If you choose to dress in this style these are the traits you project:
Organization
Good at directing other people
Think things out in advance
Appropriate
High expectations of self and others
Don't waste time
Highly competent
Confident
Appreciate ambition
Ambitious
Efficient
Decisive
Precise
Good manager
Strong
Composed
Intense
Goal oriented
Career minded
Respected and respectful
Disciplined
Keep calm and in control
Shy of showing your sexy side
Don't enjoy change

If you have the personality characteristics described in this profile you are an Achiever. You display the ability to set goals, decide how to reach them, and call on discipline to make them happen. Your style is the master organizer and you get a lot done because of this valuable skill. You are an admired professional and usually succeed. You are a woman who can keep her emotions in check when needed. You are good at directing people and have the qualities of a terrific manager. You intend to do things right the first time and you like precision. Taste is restrained, not flashy or extreme. Yours is a confident personality.

Others often view you as having it all together with seemingly effortless organization. The ability to take responsibility and display strength in a crisis makes you a valued friend and partner. You are a thinker and can be reasoned with during emotional trauma. Your ability to get things done and your sense of integrity set a fine example for your children.

As an Achiever when you lack self esteem it is expressed as a need to control. Your competence can make many people feel intimidated. By being easier on yourself you can lessen your need to appear perfect and as a result improve your relationships with others. This does not mean that you should try to be less accomplished, merely be aware that perfectionism can be counterproductive and cause turmoil in the ranks.

When you are pressured or doubt yourself, you truly dislike change. Typical of being an Achiever, you can get through any change but don't like it or look forward to it. The best gift you can give to yourself is to create a more inviting and warm appearance. This will help people feel they can approach you. When push comes to shove humans go to someone they think will understand them. You should take time from work to show your human side. I have met very few Achievers who aren't warm and kind people—you just may forget to show it sometimes.

A woman like you has a home in good order. Your decor is of quality and uncluttered. Most people of your style like being around active, fun or easy-going people at home. This balances some of your own intensity. Typically there is quality wood furniture of excellent taste in your home. If anything is broken or worn you probably get rid of it or fix it. You take good care of your things and they last a long time, which is why your taste for high quality can be very practical.

The nonverbal skills that you will find helpful in relationships are smile and touch (handshake or hug). Along with a more relaxed style of dress, the use of these tools will help you keep the admiration of others and soften the intimidation of your "perfection."

In the choice of clothes quality is important to your style. You don't need a ton of clothes. Your organizational skills will make your wardrobe of high value and versatile at the same time. To best accomplish this follow the "Time To Take Action" section on page 247.

You should never get stubborn about the old hemline you wear. If you make the change to the best skirt and jacket lengths you will not regret it. I advise you to check out all of your suits in which the jackets are too short—think of the skirt as a separate piece. A green skirt from one suit can be mixed with the black jacket of another if the hems are right. You should bite the bullet and experiment with accessories. They will make all of your clothes more valuable. You will catch on quickly once you let go of old ingrained ideas. Letting go is the hardest chore for your style, but it should be the number one priority for developing a successful image.

The work environment that allows you to shine is obviously the corporate or business world. There you will be tops at directing and organizing. It is best if you are not responsible for the detail work; your love for precision can handicap productivity. No matter how corporate your world might be communication is needed. Since communication is a two-way street, you will find more success at work if you dress in a manner that is professional, yet expresses your desire to listen to others.

It truly is exciting that there are so many differences in people. Appreciate the fact that you have an effective personality for this society. Try and appreciate the differences in others as much as you can along the way. No one is better or worse than you—only different. By the way, my mentor who taught me the ropes of business is an Achiever who went out of her way to keep me from falling on my face. She is a giving and delightful person and I always appreciated the fact that she gives because she wants to, not because she feels she should. If you are an Achiever be proud of the fact that you are the most admired professional woman of our day. You've earned all you have in the way of respect. It's who you are.

Style #3 - The Achiever

Illustration #34A   Illustration #34B   Illustration #34C

Illustration #34A
  Dress: White sheer wool bodice, red wool crepe skirt, collar and cuffs, black buttons.
  Earrings: Gold and black.
  Necklace: Gold and black.
  Hose: Charcoal.
  Shoes: Black and white.

Illustration #34B
  Suit: Charcoal worsted wool.
  Blouse: Teal silk.
  Necklace: Black and silver choker.
  Earrings: Black.
  Hose: Off-black.
  Shoes: Black.

Illustration #34C
  Jumpsuit: Mauve raw silk.
  Scarf: Mauve, olive and cream challis.
  Belt: Olive and mauve.
  Shoes: Gray.

Elements Of The Achiever's Style

<u>Proportion</u>

<u>Skirt Lengths/Styles:</u>   Classic length
                              Straight
             Long length
                              Gore
                              Straight

        Straight skirts with interesting detail on the back or side are excellent.

<u>Jacket Lengths:</u>   Long—just below rear
                        Long—finger tip
                        Long—knee

<u>Style of Jackets/</u>
      <u>Cardigans:</u>   Tailored
                        Notch lapel
                        Jewel neck
                        No lapel
                        Different color of collar

<u>Necklines:</u>   Button-up collars
                        High soft collar
                        Jewel

<u>Sleeves:</u>   Long
                        Cap

Colors

Core	Accent
Black	Red
Charcoal	White
Coffee bean brown	Teal green
Cream	Teal blue
Olive	Royal
	Mauve
	Forest green

Red, black and white is an excellent combination for this style. Owning blouses in accent colors adds a lot of versatility to basic suits.

Prints

Small paisley
Small geometric
Small herring bone
Small houndstooth
Black and white prints are excellent

Fabrics

Wool gabardine	Worsted wool
Raw silk	Washable silk
China silk	Silk jacquard
Any silk you like	Wool blends
Sheer wool	Satin
Velvet	Twills
Wool crepe	Wool challis
Soft wool flannel	Linen
Smooth textured rayon blends	

Wearing sleek and defined lines with fabrics that are tailored but not body hugging are excellent for this style.

Makeup

Use basic application of makeup only (page 118).

Lip colors: Soft red (no orange)
                  Deep rose

Hair

Neat
Classic
Up to date cut
Above shoulder in length
You can also wear a precise cut such as a blunt cut or short and longer on top. For examples see iIllustrations 34A, B and C.

Accessory Wardrobe

"Basic" refers to gold, silver, and black stone.

Necklaces: 24-inch long at least 1/4 inch thick
                    1 Each basic
            30-inch long at least 1/8 inch thick
                    1 Gold
                    1 Silver

Earrings: Nickle to quarter size, oblong
                    2 Gold
                    2 Silver
                    1 Gold with black
                    1 Silver with black

Bracelets: Bracelet watch
                    1 Gold
                    1 Silver

Pins: Silver dollar or larger
                    1 Silver with black
                    1 Gold with black
                    1 With red
                    1 With royal blue

Belts: Leather at least 1-1/2 inch thick
                    1 Black with matching buckle
                    1 Black with silver or gold buckle
                    1 Red
                    1 Cream
                    1 Black, red and white combination

<u>Shoes:</u>	Pumps
	1 Pair black
	1 Pair black/white spectator
	1 Pair olive or charcoal
	Flats
	1 Pair black
	1 Pair in an accent color
	1 Pair olive or charcoal
<u>Purses:</u>	Shoulder strap, plenty of pockets
	1 Black
	1 With olive, charcoal or cream
<u>Nylons:</u>	Charcoal
	Silver grey

<u>Detachable shoulder pads.</u>

When selecting the method you want to accessorize an outfit use the suggestions on page 107. The suggestions best for your style use three finishing accessories or only basics.

STYLE # 4 - THE ELEGANT LADY

Personality Profile

If you choose to dress in this style these are the traits you project:
Graciousness
Altruism
Love formal affairs
A true lady
Understated taste
A list maker
Proper
Love high quality
Elegant taste
Wise about people
Like society
Striking
Poised
Well mannered
Upstanding
Thoughtful
Social
Discreet
Charming
Dislike extremes
Politically savvy

If you have the personality characteristics described in this profile you are an Elegant Lady. You are the epitome of elegance and class. It does not take money to have class and you know that. You are not a woman who flaunts your good fortune or pushes it onto anyone. You are gracious and empathetic for the concerns of others. You are probably sought out for social affairs because you add stability and flair to the occasion. You are the perfect hostess for any formal event. You are admired for your understated taste. You are a woman who is assertive but not aggressive. You are a natural leader of people but rarely express a need for much recognition.

The class and appropriateness of your personality makes you capable of getting along with anyone from any walk of life as long as you are willing to roll up your sleeves along with everybody else. You are usually a very easy going and accepting friend and partner. A lot of male politicians want just your kind of woman behind them. As a parent you are understanding, concerned about education, involved and disciplined.

As an Elegant Lady when you lack self confidence it usually shows up as a lack of tolerance for the differences in others. A little of the social climbing attitude may come out in your personality. Money may become the determining factor in far too many friendships and social occasions. You will probably start to feel stressed if you get so busy that your home environment becomes disorganized. If you are feeling blue or down take the time to make a list of things to be done. The process imparts a sense of order. To counter depression when you are down, develop a more inviting appearance. Not only will it pick you up, but it will make you seem less aloof to some people who feel uneasy around you. Adopting elements from the Straight Shooter or the Gentlewoman will help you accomplish this.

The home of the Elegant Lady is elegant, tasteful and serene. A few wonderful pieces of art or furniture presented in a classy way is typical of your home. Any prints are subtle and usually dusted or neutral in color. Your home is likely to look more expensive than it is. You have a flair for decorating and for making people comfortable even in the most posh of interiors. Entertaining at home is a love of this style. Chances are as an Elegant Lady you are a wonderful cook, hostess and create a home environment to be admired.

The nonverbal skills you will find helpful in your relationships with people are touch, smile and laughter. These support your caring attitude yet break down the tentativeness some people may have of approaching you.

In the choice of clothing it is important for you to have high quality. Regardless of price, no jacket or skirt of the wrong length will look classy. Failure to mix your solid pieces will limit your elegant look and can give the impression that you always wear the same thing. You are emulated for your taste in clothes and a compliment coming from you means a great deal.

If you wear prints, I suggest them in long skirts or in scarves for versatility and to promote consistency in your look. Elegant Ladies love gems and pearls. Costume jewelry is not your style but you will have a much more appropriate style for casual affairs if you will get some basic costume jewelry in gold, silver or other metal to wear. Ivory and white, or gray and taupe are elegant color combinations. You probably love shoes and handbags and you spend good money on them. There is no need to have a different shoe or purse for every outfit; instead you should coordinate the <u>tone</u> of these accessories with the outfit.

This will help you to channel your money into wonderful pieces for your basic wardrobe.

Be sure to add scarves to your closet. You don't need to wear them in a large variety of ways; just the finish they give is elegant and feminine. If you desire a "new" look you should buy a new scarf or different colored blouse to go with something you already own. If you want a more casual look simply adopt two of the elements of the Straight Shooter. A more approachable look is easily obtained with Gentlewoman elements.

The work environment that allows you to best utilize your character is one where you are organizing people and keeping them on track. Your ability with people comes from the respect you give to them. If you are in a disorganized situation it will wear on your productivity. A world with a lot of communication needs would be great whether in a creative or corporate business. As an Elegant Lady you are a good leader and realize while a superior can make you a manager only the people you manage can make you a leader.

An Elegant Lady has the ability to deal with people from all walks of life without feeling superior in any way. Your graciousness gives people a feeling of being accepted. By the way, a loving advisor I know has a lot of the Elegant Lady in her personality. She is a minister and when self doubt creeps in she looks for people who will support her in finding her direction. Once she's refocused she can organize best on her own and she takes off again. As an Elegant Lady you can handle a lot as long as your foundation is in control. You may have been raised in the country club world, but you relate to all people. There is never a wrong time or place for "class." Be thankful that this is part of who you are.

Style #4 - The Elegant Lady

Illustration #35A   Illustration #35B   Illustration #35C

Illustration #35A

Blouse and skirt: Wine, linen blend.
Jacket: Light gray, light-weight flannel.
Brooch: Pewter with amethyst.
Earrings: Amethyst and pewter.
Hose: Charcoal gray.
Shoes: Burgundy.

Illustration #35B

Sweater and skirt: Cream marino wool knit.
Necklace: Gold with pearl.
Earrings: Gold with pearl.
Bracelet: Gold.
Hose: Ivory.
Shoes: Ivory.

Illustration #35C

Dress: Ice pink rayon crepe.
Scarf: Ice pink, teal and light yellow chiffon.
Belt: Light yellow.
Earrings: Pewter with rose quartz.
Hose: Gray.
Shoes: Soft pink.

Elements Of The Elegant Lady's Style

Proportion

Skirt Lengths/Styles: Classic length
Straight
Long length
Straight
Gore
Knife pleat
Detail at seams, waist band or back of skirts is good.

Jacket Lengths: Long—finger tip
Long—knee length
Peplum (with long straight skirt)

Style of Jackets or:
Cardigans: Shawl lapel
No lapel
"V" necked
Rounded shoulder

Necklines: Button-down the back
Scoop with broad shoulders
Jewel
Deep scoop
Drape neck
Cowl

Sleeves: Long
Cap

Mid-upper arm

Colors

Core	Accent
Light gray	Teals
Taupe	Eggplant
Cream	Ivory
Wine	Very light yellow
Beige	Ice pink
Cadet blue	

For this look to be successful you should wear colors that are alike in tone. In other words, all light and all deep tones together.

Prints

Rich-colored paisleys
Tone-on-tone prints
Cream backgrounds instead of white
Almost all solids

Fabrics

Linen	Wool gabardine
Silks	Raw silk
Cashmere	Wool crepe
Rayon crepe	Chiffon
Fine velvet	Rayon
Marino wool knit	Linen blends
Light-weight flannel	Crepe

Use sleek-laying fabrics that are nice to touch. Don't be shy of mixing your fabrics.

Makeup
Use basic application of make up only (page 118).

Lip colors: Light or deep rose

Hair

Sophisticated
Not faddish
Soft around the face
This style has a timeless look to it that adds to your elegance. For examples see illustrations 35A, B and C.

Accessory Wardrobe

"Basic" refers to gold, pewter and pearl.

Necklaces: 24-inch to 30-inch gold at least 1/16 inch
thick chain for gems
      Your favorite stone for the chain
      Diamond for the chain
18-inch multiple strand of pearls
24 to 30-inch long 1/8 inch thick
   chain
      1 Gold
      1 Pewter

Earrings: Dime size gold jacket to wear with
      1 Pair diamonds
      1 Pair pearls
Nickle to quarter size
      2 Gold
      2 Pewter

Bracelets: At least 1/4 inch wide
      1 Gold
      1 Pewter
      1 Gold bracelet watch

Pins: Larger than silver dollar
      1 Gold
      1 Pewter
      1 With pearl

<u>Belts:</u>	Pinchable leather or fabric without a buckle
	1 Cream
	1 Wine or dark navy
	1 Gray
<u>Shoes:</u>	Flats and pumps
	1 Pair each charcoal gray
	1 Pair each taupe or light gray
	1 Pair textured or two-tone in core color
<u>Purses:</u>	Textured
	1 With gray
	1 With wine or navy
<u>Nylons:</u>	Charcoal
	Silver-gray
	Cream

<u>Detachable shoulder pads</u>

When selecting the way you want to accessorize an outfit use the suggestions on page 107. The suggestions best for your style use three finishing accessories.

STYLE #5 - THE DYNAMO

Personality Profile

If you choose to dress in this style these are the traits you project:

One of a kind, unique
Originality
Dramatic
Exotic
Persuasive
Self assured
Appear confident
Realize you are special
Soft spoken or flamboyant—but noticed
Don't want to look like others
Love fashion
Like to stand out
Making an entrance sounds like fun
Love the extremes
Creative thinker
You have possibly raised clutter to an art form
Don't like conformity or uniformity
Try a lot of things and keep what is good
Have a strong presence
Always put your personal stamp on things
Adventurous
Showman, entertaining personality
Risk taker
Style is not affected by what others think
Queenly
Gregarious

Outgoing
Stimulating
Inventive
Love change
Love a good time
Often a thrill seeker
Demonstrative
Glamourous
Fantastic style

If you have the personality characteristics described in this profile you are a Dynamo. You are a dynamic woman; no ifs, ands or buts about it. You are often described as "one of a kind," and love it. As a Dynamo you have no desire or need to look like others. It isn't callousness that permits you to care little about what others think. It's simply the clear picture that you carry of who you are. Your taste is defined in your own head and rarely understood by another person. You are considered hard to second guess or buy for. You are very confident and self assured, a woman of extremes and rarely if ever a fence sitter on any issue or action.

As a Dynamo you avoid sameness, dullness or uniformity and have an outgoing, gregarious attitude. You don't admire people who fear change and stagnate in life. As a friend or partner you are tolerant of faults and ask the same respect in return. You come from an emotional frame of mind and really enjoy a lot of appreciation and recognition in your life. Friends and partners who allow you the limelight will reap many benefits. You are excellent at making changes in yourself and are usually devoted to self improvement.

When your self esteem suffers a blow your need for center stage increases. You should be aware that others also deserve to be at the center of things. Learning to be gracious and relinquishing the spotlight is a trait you will want to cultivate. You will discover that when you <u>do</u> draw back you will be admired, and you will experience aspects of people that you have missed over the years. Conversations that result will become learning experiences.

A good partner for you is one who requires little attention from others, someone quietly confident and with a mind and life of his own. A person who is reliable and takes care of detail will balance your life very well. Someone who is active but in different areas than yours will offer you opportunities for new learning. You can give this person fun and excitement and he can provide you with stability and security. You aren't the maternal type, but you are a great mother. As a mom you will always be there for your children and you don't expect perfection. Your children find you to be a good and fun friend. The Straight Shooter, Achiever, Elegant Lady, and Gentlewoman are all great friends and partners to balance your traits.

As a Dynamo you do not live in an average house or apartment. You love extremes. As a hostess you like entertaining in new and original ways. Home is either all white with minimum furnishing or has so much clutter that you have raised it to an art form. You are excellent at using odd things for different purposes. You probably love to change your furniture around.

Active listening is the number one nonverbal skill that will help you in relationships. Your power and self confidence are wonderful and positive attributes and should not be suppressed. You should make an effort, however, to let people know you care enough to listen to them.

The Dynamo is probably ahead of the fashion game but regardless of trend you will choose to wear only what is good for your defined "look." You may search and spend a lot to maintain your defined image. When you read about Elements of Style in this book it probably made perfect sense to you. Your number one priority is to learn to create your style with accessories, not with individual outfits. This will allow you more versatility with everything you buy. If you wish to enhance your approachability, you only have to add a few elements of the All American or Elegant Lady. You could also accomplish this by limiting your finishing accessories to three and wearing less black around your face. These suggestions all help to bring your larger-than-life image down to a more understood and therefore a more approachable one.

The work environment in which you as a Dynamo shine involves dealing with people, sharing of ideas and requires the art of persuasion. You need to have a voice in what is to be done or how it is to be done. Communication areas are terrific for you but you must be sure to remember that listening is half of communication. You encounter risk with confidence, but should avoid any job that requires you to do detail work. You will work well within the creative world and you may discover easier acceptance of your personality in this environment than in the corporate world. If you are asked to brainstorm or solve problems in a creative way you will enjoy it and be successful at your work.

The Dynamo reflects the spice of life and when you have an important relationship with a stable, down-to-earth kind of person then there is no stopping you—a woman of flair. Remember, in order to be really good at center stage you have to show appreciation for all the people supporting you on stage and those behind the scenes. By the way, a dear friend of mine is all Dynamo in an artistic world. There is no one who compares with her readiness to accept others for who they are and for always having something constructive and positive to say. A Dynamo simply needs appreciation for who she is. Surrendering the limelight to a Dynamo is a small sacrifice considering what she gives in return. If you are a Dynamo let it be okay for you to need outward reinforcement. Everyone wants it; you just ask for it up front. That's who you are.

Style #5 - The Dynamo

Illustration #36A   Illustration #36B   Illustration #36C

Illustration #36A
Dress: Emerald, wool jersey.
Scarf: Black, emerald, cobalt and gold, silk.
Belt: Black elastic with emerald and gold flower.
Earrings: Emerald and gold.
Hose: Charcoal.
Shoes: Black.

Illustration #36B
Duster and skirt: Magenta wool gabardine.
Blouse: White satin.
Hat: Black with magenta detail.
Earrings: Black and silver.
Belt: Black with silver and magenta colored stone.
Hose: Off-black.
Shoes: Black.

Illustration #36C
Blouse: Light bronze with black leather detail.
Pants: Black tissue suede.
Earrings: Bronze beads on black base.
Belt: Black leather tube with bronze chain.
Boots: Black.

Elements Of The Dynamo's Style

Proportion

<u>Skirt Lengths/Styles:</u> Classic length

                             Straight

                             Tulip

               Mini length

                             Gore

                             Straight

                             Tulip

                             Trumpet

               Long length

                             Gore

                             Circle

                             Straight

                             Trumpet

<u>Jacket Lengths:</u>   Waist length

                       Long—just below rear

                       Long—finger tip

                       Long—knee length

                       Duster (with pants or long straight
                         skirt)

<u>Style of Jackets or</u>
        <u>Cardigans:</u>   Scarf lapels

                       Fancy lapels

                       Print jackets

                       Wide lapels

                       Unique styles

                       Very broad shoulder pads

Necklines:	Unique collars
	Jewel
	Drape
	High turtle
	Necklines that can be worn several
	ways

Sleeves:	Long pushed to three quarter length
	Long
	Cutout sleeveless

Colors

Core	Accent
Red	Hot pink
Gold	Magenta
Bright purple	Emerald green
Black	Chrome yellow
White	Pewter
Royal blue	Bronze
Fuchsia	
Cornflower blue	

If you like the color and it's bright, then it's right for this look. Don't be shy about mixing any of these colors.

Prints

Bright and bold dramatic prints
Strong geometric
Large floral
Large paisleys
Big stripes

Asymmetrical prints
Jungle prints
Hand-painted original prints
Large black and white prints

Fabrics

Jersey	Leather
Wool gabardine	Linen
Jacquard	Hammered satin
Tissue suede	Raw silk
Jersey	Lamé
Cotton blends	Rayon blends
Heavy mummy silks	Challis

The lay of your fabric is so important to your style that you will want to be sure it will maintain its look. All of your fabrics mix with the use of accessories.

Makeup

Use the basic application (page 118) for work and casual, glamour for evening (page 121).

Lip colors: Fire engine red
Burgundy
Raisin
Bright and dark colors

Hair

Asymmetrical
Unique
Dramatic
Latest in style

You should be able to alter the look of the cut. Try different colors or a strip of a color somewhere in the hair. Use hair pieces for extra length and variety. For examples see illustrations 36A, B and C.

Accessory Wardrobe

"Basic" refers to copper, gold, bronze, silver and pewter.

<u>Necklaces:</u> 30-inch long, at least 1/2 inch thick
           1 Each basic
16-inch collar 1 inch thick
           1 of the basics
30-inch long
           1 in combination of basics
30-inch long pendant or multiple chains
           2 of the basics

<u>Earrings:</u> Quarter size
           1 Each basic
           1 Each accent color
Dangle or hoop
           1 Each basic
           1 Each accent color

<u>Bracelets:</u> Bangles or cuffs
           1 Each basic
           1 Black

<u>Scarf pins:</u> 1 Silver
1 Gold
    A scarf pin is a large brooch with a hole in it to pull scarves through.

<u>Pins</u>:	At least silver dollar size
	1 Each basic mixed with other
	stones and metals

<u>Belts</u>: All belts at least 2 inches wide
    Black with gold or silver
    Black - buckle also black
    Red leather
    1 Each accent color
1 Large detachable buckle in combination
of basics
Leather straps to use with buckle

<u>Shoes</u>: Pumps
    1 Pair black
    1 Pair gray two-tone
Low heel textured
    1 Pair black
Flats
    1 Pair black
    1 Pair bright accent color
Boots soft leather with heel
    1 pair black

<u>Purses</u>: Large soft leather
    1 Black with bright accent colors
    1 two-tone black
    1 two-tone gray

<u>Nylons</u>: Off-black
Charcoal
Silver-gray
Cream

Textured (worn with long skirts for
evening).

<u>Detachable Shoulder Pads.</u>

<u>Sleevebands</u>

When selecting the way you want to accessorize an outfit use the suggestions on page 107. The suggestions best for your style use one large finishing accessory (any occasion) or three finishing accessories (casual) or more than three finishing accessories (any occasion).

STYLE # 6 - THE INDIVIDUALIST

Personality Profile

If you choose to dress in this style these are the traits you project:

Right brain thinker all the way
Nonconformist
Off beat
Free spirit
You are your own woman first and foremost
You don't announce your individuality, you live it
Private person
Live by your own time clock
Noncompetitive with others
Unrushed, often late but get there
Money is not a big priority
Love thrift and flea markets
Not into new and shiny, prefer unique
Don't like rules and principles
Create your own look
Often an activist
Love interest over chicness
Not rigid or routine
The rebel in you may close you off from others
Intriguing
Rebellious
Often artistic or highly creative
Talented
Walks her own road, even if alone
Shows mood swings freely
Often active in environmental issues

If you have the personality characteristics described in this profile you are an Individualist. Your style of woman is her own person first, last and foremost; a free spirit. Individuality is practiced quietly and usually with profound stubbornness. Your style lives on your own time clock due to your strong right brain way of living and thinking.

As an Individualist you buck rules and regulations. You have the heart of the rebel and don't like to be dictated to. You probably balked at being classified in this book because you feel it makes you a conformist. This couldn't be further from the truth. Your essence is nonconformity. You will not buy an outfit from a store window. You probably don't read fashion magazines, and every look you create is a reflection of a mood or a side of yourself.

Individualists make a difference in the quality of life. Every Individualist is different—some radical, some quite shy. What they have in common is the love of differences, creative abilities that are admired and a keen awareness of social and environmental issues. In fact many Individualists are activists because they have the courage to buck the system.

A private person, your style often is considered to be rebellious, a trait that can close you off from groups. A good partner or friend for the Individualist is someone who is flexible, introspective and respects the privacy of others. You have to make an effort to build relationships with others because your independent life makes people feel they are intruding. You enjoy solving problems on your own but you should let those whom you love know that your penchant for doing things yourself is not meant to exclude them, or to express your distrust of them. You are more right brain oriented, thus talking about problems (left brain activity) doesn't work as well for you.

As a parent you are not bound to rules and believe in experimentation. Children may see you as irresponsible about left brain activities such as bill paying, organization and punctuality. But you will remember the rebelliousness of your own youth and can be a terrific listener for your children. As a mother you set a great example for appreciating beauty and fighting for what you believe in.

As an Individualist when you lack self esteem you become scattered and undirected often exhibiting rebelliousness and rejecting conformity. You may close yourself off from others and try to place blame for failure on other people. You may be moody in the best and worst way. No one can be more thrilled about simple things or bluer than your style.

As an Individualist, you should be aware that what you do affects persons who may not be comfortable with your roller coaster moods because they feel out of control, unable to help. Stormy transitional times are part of your growth and development. Being alone can be productive for your ingenious right brain problem-solving abilities.

Usually your home is a crazy quilt of textures and styles, filled with mementos. You are not too big on the shiny and new. You probably prefer things that have a story or memory attached to them. As a hostess, you always have an experience in store for your guests. You love the off-beat and different; a portion of the decor in your home probably came from flea markets and thrift stores.

A lot of layers and textures and original combinations are terrific for your style of hair. There is only one rule I try hard to get the Individualist to adopt— that is proportion. Without a clear decision to do this you will hinder your creative process. Most Individualists are visual and once you see the difference that proportion brings into your appearance, you will probably adopt it easily. No clothing combination can be wrong for your style. The use of scarves and belts will allow you to create original combinations most effectively.

Your biggest misconception is that you don't need other people to be successful. Of course this is not true, but it does show up in your tendency to avoid accepting criticism. If you work on eye contact, body language and decrease the off-beat look of your clothing you will find less conflict and more understanding from people who can make or break your career.

The work environment in which you will shine offers creative outlets, time and space to work alone and a minimum of rules or time constraints. The corporate world is the opposite of your personality and you should consider the long-term effects this world may have on your happiness and self esteem should you elect to work in this environment. Good communication is vital if you are to survive in most jobs or careers today. If you are able to have your own creative business, you will need to either make the effort to listen, care and understand others or you will need to hire someone to do it. The Individualist's unwillingness to do this is one of the main reasons so many famous artists, authors and inventors left this world as paupers.

Because you are off-beat and different there will always be people who will be uncomfortable with you and your ways. These are usually people who admire self control. Their criticism stems from their own lack of self esteem and and inability to control you. They see you as a threat. You do not need to be a conformist to get along but you do need to work on understanding others.

It is worthwhile for the rest of us to try to see things through the eyes of an Individualist once in a while. By the way, my Individualist clients who have chosen to work actively on understanding the views of others have reported a lot more pleasure and less stress with life in return for their efforts. One client said, "I still have a look that is all my own but now others seem to relate to me better. That can only help." But never let anyone tell you that your individualistic traits are "wrong." They can't be. They make up who you are!

Style #6 - The Individualist

Illustration #37A   Illustration #37B   Illustration #37C

Illustration #37A

    Dress: Khaki heavy gauze.
    Necklace: Pewter and bronze.
    Earrings: Copper.
    Belt: Khaki, cognac and olive.
    Tights: Brown.
    Shoes: Khaki and brown.

Illustration #37B

    Jacket: Rust with chartreuse tweed and fuschia plaid, coarse wool blend.
    Skirt: Medium brown heavy cotton.
    Mock turtleneck: Chartreuse rayon.
    Scarf: Chartreuse with fuschia and dark brown.
    Brooch: Antique gold with fuschia and amber stones.
    Belt: Dark brown with fuschia.
    Bracelet: Copper and antique gold combined.
    Hat: Rust.
    Boots: Dark brown with copper chain.

Illustration 37C

    Shirt: Khaki raw silk.
    Turtleneck: Curry cotton.
    Pants: Dark purple, wide-wale corduroy.
    Jacket/sweater: Olive cotton and acrylic coarse knit.
    Earrings: Dark purple feathers.
    Belt: Black.
    Bracelets: Copper.
    Man's tie: Curry, purple and black.
    Hair band: Black.
    Shoes: Brown and black.

Elements Of The Individualist's Style

Proportion

Skirt Lengths/Styles: Mini length
                              Gored
                              Full skirts
                              Straight
                 Long length
                              Drop yoke
                              Gored
                              Full
                              Straight

Uneven hems, boot skirts and period styles are great.

Jacket Lengths: Waist length
                             Long—finger tip
                             Long—knee length
                             Duster

Style of Jackets or
       Cardigans: Oversized of any style
                             Styles from different eras

Necklines: Collars easy to layer with
                             Huge turtles
                             Huge cowls
                             Deep "V" necks
                             Huge scoops
                             Collars of different eras

Sleeves: Long pushed to three-quarter length
                  Long
                  Sleeveless

Colors

Core   Accent
Olive   Purple
Curry   Coral
Khaki   Fuchsia
Rust   Chartreuse
Cognac   Dark orange
Bottle green   Neons
Black
Unique browns

The mixing of interesting colors is a great look for the individualist. If it's original or off-beat it's great.

Prints

Dark or neon color prints
Coarse textures
Odd raised textures
Unconventional prints
Abstract prints
Menswear stripe
Antique florals
Era prints (such as dots of the 40's)
Hand-painted original prints
Combining two different prints

Fabrics

Gauze	Heavy cotton
Ribbed knits	Cut velvet
Suede	Rayon
Burlap	Canvas
Challis	Leather
Raw silk	Wool gabardine
Wide wale corduroy	Coarse textures

Natural fibers are best for this style.

Makeup

Use the basic (page 118), glamour or casual (page 121) application as the mood suits you.

<u>Lip colors:</u>   Oranges
Corals
Brownish red
Dark colors

Hair

Frizzy
Wild
Versatile
Different in color and style

You can easily wear a style that is a little rebellious. Try wigs of different colors. For examples see illustrations 37A, B and C.

Accessory Wardrobe

"Basic" refers to antique gold, pewter, copper and bronze.

Necklaces: At least 30 inches long, 1/4 inch thick
multiple chains and pendants
    1 Each basic
16 to 30 inches long each at least 1/2 inch
thick
    2 Unique, mixed in with a basic

Earrings: Quarter size
    3 Pair with a basic in each
Dangles
    3 Pair with a basic in each

Bracelets: Cuffs and bangles in each basic

Pins: Antique or unique
    3 With a basic in each
    3 With accent color in each

Belts: At least 1-1/2 inch wide, textured or unique
style
    2 Black
    2 Brown
    2 Others in accent colors

Shoes: Flats
    1 Pair black
    1 Pair olive or khaki

Pumps
    1 Pair black
Boots, low heel, soft leather
    1 Pair black
    1 Pair brown,

<u>Purses:</u>   Oversize print or textures
    1 Light colored
    1 Dark colored

<u>Nylons:</u>   Off-black
Charcoal
Silver-gray
Textured for short or long skirts with
    flats (not appropriate for work)

<u>Shoulder Pads</u>

<u>Sleevebands.</u>

When selecting the way you want to accessorize an outfit use the suggestions on page 107. The suggestions best for your style use three or more finishing accessories.

PROFILE #7 - THE GENTLEWOMAN

Personality Profile

If you choose to dress in this style these are the traits you project:

Inviting and warm
Kind
Soft of skin, heart, manner and look
Intelligent
Understanding of others
People come first
Love all living things
Love a homemade lifestyle
Like a clean house but it looks lived in
Like antique and estate sales
Love flowers and gardening
Buy things you love rather than always need
A good listener
Generous
Enjoy being at home with family or dream of it
A smiling, content and peaceful person
Make others feel comfortable
Love mementos
Subtle
Fulfilled as a woman
Compassionate
Empathetic
Sentimental
Easy going
Patient with kids and animals
People-clever

Considerate
Rooted
Sincere

If you have the personality characteristics described in this profile you are a Gentlewoman. You are a woman who exhibits remarkable intuition. You live for the understanding of humans, animals and all living things. There is no style more intelligent or more understanding when it concerns people. You are non-threatening and approachable. Often you can get people to do what you want and they are happy doing it. You are an excellent communicator because of your ability and desire to understand and put yourself in the shoes of others.

As the Gentlewoman you are fascinated by the beauty of the outdoors, the treasures in an estate sale and the love of animals and children. You are admired for your patience and caring and you prioritize living things over money, power, etc.

In a friend or partner you will find happiness with those who share your care for living things and who don't need to dominate or control. If people dislike your feminine ways they probably won't appreciate you and you will shine better without them in your life. As a parent you are the picture of the loving mother. You love the role of a parent and all that goes with it. You are a woman who will teach your children that family comes first.

When you lack self esteem it usually is demonstrated by what might be labeled a nagging attitude or a need to give sympathy or pity. These negative traits come out only on occasions. As a whole you are a positive, loving, caring individual.

You often have the misconception that your femininity may injure your business relationships. In fact, your personality in business is usually very successful when true to yourself and your femininity. Your success stems from the ability to listen to others and will carry you far in business affairs.

Because you put the people in your life first, your home may have a slightly rumpled and lived-in look, but is usually quite clean. You will have children's pictures on the refrigerator and your first child's baby blanket in the attic. You probably love decorating and take pride in your home. Most Gentlewomen either like rooms with a lot of light or rich Victorian decor.

The nonverbal skills that will most help you in relationships with others are tone of voice, facial expressions and body language. You must learn to use these skills to be effective at managing situations in which emotions interfere with sound decisions.

You admire beauty that is soft, not harsh. Nice skin is something you should work diligently to achieve. You buy things because you love them, then have difficulty finding ways to wear them. Haphazard shopping results in a wardrobe of many clothes and nothing to wear. Your best accessories are brooches and scarves. The number one priority in your wardrobe should be to clean out that closet. You probably have trouble throwing things away because everything has a memory. Do yourself a favor and get rid of your high school clothes and those which don't fit your style.

At work you will enjoy an environment that allows you to help others. Working for an Achiever will give you the opportunity for mediation. You will be appreciated for being able to understand the pressures Achievers put on themselves. The more communication you have with people the better you will be at your own work. The Gentlewoman is not great at conflict resolution. You will probably be much happier working in your quiet way to prevent problems from happening through good communication.

If you are still shy about showing your true feminine side because you hold a powerful position, I hope you will buy a few books that can clarify for you the difference in feminine and masculine power. For a Gentlewoman to try and project masculine strength is to go against the nature of who she is. Very few of my clients who have traits of the Gentlewoman believed how much more successful they could be by being themselves until they tried it. By the way, the friend whose opinion I most often listen to is a Gentlewoman. She is a successful and respected manager in a major corporation in the computer industry. She has no problem being taken seriously and is considered by those who know her to be quick-witted and assertive...and she loves to wear lace. Learning the power and confidence that dressing in this style can bring is truly an eye opener for women. Rejoice in your femininity.

Style #7 - The Gentlewoman

Illustration #38A   Illustration #38B   Illustration #38C

Illustration #38A

Jacket and skirt: Dark purple rayon crepe with velvet lapels.
Blouse: Cream silk.
Earrings: Antique gold.
Brooch: Antique gold with purple and pink colored stones.
Hose: Charcoal.
Shoes: Navy.

Illustration #38B

Dress: Light aqua soft cotton knit.
Scarf: Dusty rose, pink, blue and light aqua silk.
Belt: Dusty rose.
Earrings: Gold.
Hose: Light gray.
Shoes: Light gray.

Illustration #38C

Sweater: Burgundy angora.
Skirt: Mallard, burgundy, soft pink on pearl gray background, chiffon.
Scarf: Pearl gray, soft lace.
Brooch: Silver with burgundy stone.
Earrings: Silver and burgundy.
Hose: Gray.
Shoes: Gray.

Elements Of The Gentlewoman's Style

Proportion

Skirt Lengths/Styles: Classic length
                                  Straight
                      Long length
                                  Drop yoke
                                  Gore
                                  Straight
                                  Soft pleat
                                  Knife pleat
                                  "V" front
                                  Back pleat or slit in straight
                                  Full, any style

Jacket Lengths: Waist length (with long skirts only)
                               Long—just below rear
                               Long—finger tip
                               Peplum

Style of Jackets or
       Cardigans: Shawl
                       High necked

Necklines: High soft necks
                     Drape
                     Scoop
                     Jewel
                     Shawl
                     Notch collars

Sleeves: Long
Elbow length
Long pushed to three-quarter length
Cap

Colors

Core	Accent
Cream	Soft pink
Burgundy	Mallard green
Ivory	Lavender
Pearl gray	Gray blue
Mauve	Light aqua
Dark purples	Dusty light colors

Dusty or deep rich colors are best for this look.

Prints

Victorian prints
Antique prints
Floral
Paisleys in burgundy shades
All pastel prints

Fabrics

Silk	Rayon
Cashmere	Angora
Soft lace	Chiffon
Raw silk	Wool gabardine
Cotton knits	Tissue linen
Sheer wool	Soft crepes
Cotton	Velvet

Use flowing and soft fabrics. If it feels yummy to you—it's you.

Makeup

Use basic application (page 118) of makeup for office or evening; casual application (page 121) for a casual look.

Lip colors: Mauves
                 Roses
                 Soft pinks
                 Clear gloss

Hair

Long (or short with length on top)
Soft and wavy
Highlights.
No angular styles

Do not have it cut in too many layers so that it can still be pulled back. For examples see illustrations 38A, B and C.

Accessory Wardrobe

"Basic" refers to gold, pearls and antique gold

Necklaces: 18-inch string of pearls
24-inch chain 1/16 inch thick gold with
pearl pendant
24 to 30-inch chain 1/8 inch thick
    1 Antique gold
    1 Gold

Earrings: Dime to quarter size
    1 Oval shaped with pearl
    1 Other with pearl
    2 Gold
    2 Antique gold
Drop
    1 Each basic

Bracelets: Charm or dangle at least 1/4 inch thick
    1 Gold with pearl
    1 With antique gold

Pins: 1 Gold with pearl
1 Antique gold
3 Others of choice

Belts: 1-1/2 inch wide, soft pinchable leather with
matching buckles or no buckle
    1 Navy
    1 Cream
    1 Burgundy

                    1 Pink

Shoes: Pumps
                      1 Pair taupe or gray
                      1 Pair navy or burgundy
              Flats
                      1 Pair taupe or gray
                      1 Pair navy or burgundy

Purses: 1 With navy
              1 With taupe or gray
              Fabric purses with dusty prints are a good
              option

Nylons: Cream
              Silver-gray
              Charcoal

Detachable Shoulder pads

Sleevebands

         When selecting the way you want to accessorize an
outfit use the suggestions on page 107. The suggestions
best for your style use two finishing accessories (for
casual) or three finishing accessories (for office and
evening).

STYLE # 8 - THE INNOCENT

Personality Profile

If you choose to dress in this style these are the traits you project:

Girl next door
Sweet
Cute
Pretty
Naive
Have trouble throwing anything away
Like a natural habitat
Dislike black
Love pastel colors
Love the pristine
Spring and summer are your favorite seasons
Often seen as naive, innocent, inexperienced
Fresh looking
Coquettish
Idealistic
Cooperative
Often shy
Often perky
Princess-like
Whimsical
Romantic about life
Gentle emotions
Courteous
Love animals and children
Maternal

If you have the personality characteristics described in this profile you are an Innocent. As the Innocent, you are the wonderful girl next door who is loved by everybody. You are sweet, gentle, kind and very good with children. You are soft of skin, manner, voice and heart, equipped with a trusting outlook on life. You love flowers and spring time. Your style is romantic about life and love. You are usually good with arts and crafts and like sewing and cooking new and different things. You probably have a cat as a pet instead of a dog.

You are a woman who is probably a little shy. You may also have a coquettish way about you. You are the kind of woman men want to take home to meet mom and dad. As an Innocent it is highly likely that you love home, kids, pets and family.

Men usually want to protect you and love your friendliness and softness. You are a non-threatening personality and this causes people to treat you more kindly.

Friends and partners who appreciate things done for them and don't take advantage of your thoughtfulness are excellent for your Innocent personality. There seem to be two types of people to whom you are drawn. One is the domineering and controlling type. Usually the attraction is based on the opinion that he appears to be someone who will take care of you. The wonder and refreshing innocence that you portray can be lost with constant criticism. You must be sure that if you choose a domineering partner that he is positive and productive of your growth and self love.

The second type of partner to whom you may be attracted is the man who is kind, understanding, reliable, practical, down-to-earth and often athletic. The Straight Shooter, The All American, The Gentlewoman, are all excellent partners and friends for your refreshing personality.

As a parent you will probably grow up with your kids and give them a great example of compassion and how to get along with others. You are an old-fashioned mom who is often the room mother in your children's classroom.

When your style of woman lacks self esteem you become more little girl-like and withdrawn. This makes you someone who people worry about and often pity. You may very well become angry with people who have used or abused your kindness. Such experiences may lead you to become less trusting. Normally, you are such a warm and loving individual that if you are around people who appreciate your naivete, you will be a wonderful supporter and a gift to their lives.

When I was working in the South I met many Southern women who had a lot of the Innocent style in their personality. They were masters at getting men on their side. When men see the Innocent they see their sisters or childhood friends. This inspires a level of trust that many other types never obtain.

Your home probably has a touch of country or a little lace, maybe a collection of dolls or glassware. Pastels probably prevail in your decor as well as ruffles, pillows, patchwork and cross stitch. You may love to fuss around the house and create a pristine, inviting environment.

The nonverbal skills that will most help you in dealing with others is the handshake and erect, confident body posture. You can keep the wonder of your innocence and still be respected for your intelligence. These skills will help you do just that.

Your style of woman never wears black or anything too sexy, blatant or obvious. The essence of your beauty is soft lovely skin and clear eyes. You usually buy something because you love it and worry later about what it will go with. A lot of your choices hang in the closet—unworn for years. You should begin by eliminating any pieces in the wrong proportion. Then you should buy some solid jackets, blouses and skirts to create outfits. Having the wrong proportions is the reason you haven't found the right item to put with your "love" purchases.

In your image at work your biggest concern should be to limit the little girl look at the office. One way to do this is to wear jackets over your dresses and skirts. You may add a touch of lace to your outfit and you will still be appropriate. It is also true to your style to wear the long dress length and flat comfortable shoes. If you do have to dress in suits, I always suggest the waist length jacket with printed or matching long skirts. If you feel that you are not taken seriously when you want to be, or that too many see your innocence as a ploy, it may be beneficial for you to adopt a few of the elements of the Gentlewoman or the Elegant style.

The career at which you will shine the most is one in which you are working with healthy children or animals. You will also do well in a job that allows you to serve people in a positive environment. Your big heart makes working with the sick or abused often too difficult. It is imperative that you learn to use the word "No" or you will be taken advantage of in business. You will be better off in a world in which you are asked to communicate with others in nonconflicting ways. Having time to do your work without constant requests or interruptions is also very important. If you put yourself in a strong corporate or creative world you will loose some of your innocence.

If you are a woman of this style or would like to adopt some of the attributes of this style, you will embrace the wonder and joy of being an intelligent adult who has chosen to not let life harden you in any way. This does not mean you are a door mat or a push over. It means that you have chosen a path closer to the old beliefs of our society and it can be a wonderful life. You will want to be clear about your definition of success. If you push yourself into the social definition of success, you risk losing a lot of your wonder and trust. Many Gentlewoman, Elegant Lady and All American personalities also have qualities of the Innocent.

By the way, I have an Innocent style client who has made teacher of the year three times and is highly respected for her creative and effective teaching techniques. She is 38 years old and is in the process of publishing a reading program that has been purchased by a major publisher. She guards her innocence by hiring professionals to take care of personal business needs. Don't let anybody tell you that it is wrong to be innocent. It's who you are.

Style #8 - The Innocent

Illustration #39A   Illustration #39B   Illustration #39C

Illustration #39A
> **Blouse:** Soft pink, ivory and seafoam green organza.
> **Split skirt:** Soft pink with seafoam green organza lace.
> **Belt:** Seafoam green.
> **Necklace:** Gold with pearl colored heart.
> **Earrings:** Pearl with gold.
> **Hose:** Silver gray.
> **Shoes:** Print ivory and pink.

Illustration #39B
> **Dress:** White and navy stripe with a crisp cotton collar.
> **Pin:** Cameo, gold with rose.
> **Earrings:** Rose.
> **Hose:** Cream.
> **Shoes:** Navy.

Illustration #39C
> **Skirt:** Pearl gray rayon crepe.
> **Jacket:** Pearl gray rayon crepe with peach crisp lace collar.
> **Pin:** Silver bow.
> **Earrings:** Silver.
> **Hose:** Silver gray.
> **Shoes:** Peach.

Elements Of The Innocent's Style

Proportion

Skirt Lengths/Styles: Long length
                        Drop yoke
                        Full
                        Soft gathered
                        Flowing
                        Soft pleats
                        Gore

Jacket Lengths: Waist length
                        Long—just below rear

Style of Jackets or
     Cardigans: "W" at waistband
                        Lace lapels and collars
                        Waiter's style
                        Wide shawl
                        Soft, round shoulders
                        Flowing fabric
                        Button closed

Necklines: Square lace
                        Round lace
                        Peter Pan
                        Cut out neck
                        Soft turtle
                        Scrunch collar

Sleeves:	Puffed shoulder
	Long
	Mid-upper arm
	Elbow length

Colors

Core	Accent
Deep navy	Dusty blue
Ivory	Ice pink
White	Mint green
Soft pink	Medium pink
Pearl gray	Seafoam green
	Rose
	Soft peach

The only pinks and blues not great for this style are the bright and electric tones.

Prints

Gingham
Thin stripes
Small florals
Wavy solids with white or cream lace

Fabrics

Crisp cotton	Rayon crepe
Crepe blends	Polyester crepe
Organza	Crisp lace
Voile	Raw silk
Angora	Chiffon
Washable silk	Denim

Any cotton blend

Mixing crisp lace with soft fabrics is a nice touch. Denim and lace is also a great look for this style.

Makeup

In addition to the basic application (page 118) of makeup try the casual option (page 121) for a fresh look.

Lip Colors: Light pinks
                Pink tone gloss

Hair

Curly
Full
Jaw to chin length or shorter
Bangs pulled back a little on one side

A young style with which hair accessories can easily be worn. For examples see illustrations 39A, B and C.

Accessory Wardrobe

"Basics" refers to pearls, gold and silver.

Necklaces: 18-inch gold chain at least 1/16 inch thick
18-inch string of pearls
24 inch chain at least 1/8 inch thick
    1 Gold
    1 Silver
2 small lockets or pendants

Earrings: Dime to quarter size
    2 Gold
    2 Gold with pearl
    2 Silver

Bracelets: 1/16 to 1/4-inch thick, light weight
    1 Gold
    1 With antique gold

Pins: Quarter size or larger
    1 Gold with pearl
    1 Gold
    1 Silver
    3 Others with accent color

Belts: Pinchable leather, at least 2 inches wide,
matching buckles
    1 Cream
    1 White
    2 Navy

<u>Shoes:</u>   Pumps
                        1 Pair navy
                        1 Pair taupe or gray
                Flats
                        1 Pair navy
                        1 Pair taupe or gray
                        1 Pair black patent

<u>Purses:</u>   1 Navy
                1 Taupe or gray

<u>Nylons:</u>   Cream
                Silver-gray
                Charcoal
                Navy blue

With a long navy skirt you can wear cream hose (with a white blouse or white lace at neck) or navy hose with navy shoes.

<u>Detachable Shoulder Pads</u>

<u>Sleevebands</u>

When selecting the way you want to accessorize an outfit use the suggestions on page 107. The suggestions best for your style use three finishing accessories (office or evening) or two finishing accessories (casual).

STYLE #9 - THE KNOCKOUT

Personality Profile

If you choose to dress in this style these are the traits you will project:

Have a nice body and are proud of it
Use your body to every advantage
Prefer men over women
Men respond to you
Women are often critical or curious about you
Being sexy is fun
Vibrant
Health is to keep your body beautiful
Love make up
Viewed by many as super confident
Very confident of yourself as a woman
Happy about being a woman
Vivacious
Often the life of the party
Clothes often become your entire statement
Eager for attention
Sexy lady
Head turner
Love to flirt
Alluring
Desirable
Glittering
Love the night life
Exuberant
Seductive
Luscious

If you have the personality characteristics described in this profile you are a Knockout. Sexy, alluring and vibrant, you are super confident as a woman. You love to show off your figure more than anything else. As a Knockout you may be voluptuous or model thin, but you find your body to be the essence of beauty. You are a woman who understands how to get a man's attention and has no regrets about it. You are a wonderful flirt and a blast at any party. You love night life and know the hot spots in town. You are probably quitesensual and probably view sex as healthy and fun. This does not mean cheap or easy, but unfortunately when you choose to dress in the style of the Knockout, people are apt to consider you easy. Our cultural etiquette says that sexy is for the home. Women have worked so hard in America for equal opportunity that they have labeled "sexy" as demeaning. The truth is other women feel threatened when they meet your alluring personality.

In different parts of Europe sexy is interpreted as a zest for life and women of your style are not so harshly judged. A trip to Europe could bring memorable romance into your life. Because yours is the least accepted of the styles in our society it is important for you to understand how your style is interpreted. Understanding the views of others will help you to be more satisfied with yourself and less upset with how you are treated. You will feel more understood if you are willing to adopt a look that embodies the aspects of the Knockout but is considered more appropriate.

It goes without saying that men are always attracted to you and you often fulfill adolescent fantasies. The best partner for your style is one who admires you for traits other than your sexiness. To attract this kind of person I advise my Knockout clients to adopt two to three elements of a style that has characteristics they admire. If you do this you will be able to develop a more committed relationship with a man. Trust me, you will not lose your alluring qualities. You have wonderful winning traits that can be completely overshadowed by the seductive way you dress. When it comes to choosing women friends you should look for the most accepting people you can find. Women who exude a lot of confidence and women who are honest, direct and frank are wonderful friends for you. Because you may often have problems with other women talking behind your back, the establishment of strong bonds with females who don't feel competitive with you is of terrific value.

As a parent you love and cherish your children. Many Knockouts take on Gentlewoman or Elegant Lady qualities after they become mothers because they experience an unconditional love that softens them.

When you lack self confidence you become competitive with other women when it comes to men. This can put you in some negative or abusive relationships. The answer for you in this dilemma is to adopt some of the style of the Elegant Lady or the Straight Shooter and you will regain confidence because of the positive way you will be treated.

Your home is either earthy with no real decor or it is sleek and contemporary with a lot of white, chrome and glass. You usually have a clean house when company comes but live in disarray. As a hostess you prefer to go out to entertain.

The Knockout personality can range from the earthy and almost cowgirl type to the evening, glitzy type. You may wear skin tight jeans, huggy short skirts or plunging necklines. Your body determines the clothes. But you can show off your shape without having clothes that hug you tightly. Shopping to show off your body without regard for the whole image creates a spotty wardrobe. You may have a huge selection of clothes which isn't necessary. If you were to get some good basics you could have money to put into a head-turning outfit for a special occasion.

Dressing up for evenings and holidays is the time for you to let your full style shine through. But makeup is the biggest fashion mistake of the Knockout. More is not better. Glamour, vibrancy and glitz can be shown in a lot of other ways that don't leave the poor impression that too much makeup gives.

The earthy Knockout style is best adopting the elements of the Straight Shooter or All American. The glitzy Knockout style is best adopting the Elegant Lady elements. Whether you are the more earthy or the more glitsy Knockout elements of the Gentlewoman can be very effective to use.

You can find happiness in a creative environment because the people working there are more apt to accept you as you are. You should take a look at the different profiles and which work environments the different styles shine in. If you want to be in one of these environments you should simply adopt some of the ideal style for that world. The corporate world can be fun but you will be judged too big of a risk to have much success climbing the ladder. A job working in communications would be great for you if you temper your style to be more approachable and reliable.

Yours is a style that other women, out of insecurity and fear, have labeled in negative ways. These women feel protective of their men when you are around. It is tough to find people who can see beyond the strong stereotype this culture has given your style. If you would like to develop relationships based on your other assets you will want to tone down your sexy style. If you don't have a desire to adjust your style, that's fine. Do, however, take responsibility for the interpretation of others. The general opinion that a sexy woman is predatory is one you will have to live with if you decide not to modify your style. You have so much vibrancy and life to give, altering your style may offer you the chance to give it.

By the way, an executive producer of documentaries who is a Knockout style is a client of mine. She wasn't getting the grants and assistance she wanted and felt she deserved. She adopted the Elegant Lady style for work in every element but color and prints. For two years she has called me dozens of times to tell my how effective this adaptation has been for her in her association with people. She also has made two acquaintances into friends—the type of people with whom she always wanted to associate. When I asked her if she felt as if she had sacrificed anything in her life by adopting the Elegant Lady style, she said, "No way, I've found another part of me. When I'm out on the town I'm sexier than ever and enjoy it more."

Style #9 - The Knockout

Illustration #40A   Illustration #40B   Illustration #40C

Illustration #40A

Dress: Black and hot yellow, jersey knit.
Earrings: Black.
Belt: Black.
Bracelet: Black.
Hose: Skin-tone.
Shoes: Yellow.

Illustration #40B

Suit: Electric pink wool crepe.
Earrings: Black and silver.
Hose: Charcoal.
Shoes: Black

Illustration #40C

Blouse: Silver satin.
Pants: Hot turquoise knit.
Belt: Electric red with silver buckle.
Earrings: Electric red.
Bracelets: Electric red, silver and turquiose.
Shoes: Electric red.

Elements Of The Knockout's Style

<u>Proportion</u>

<u>Skirt Lengths/Styles:</u> Classic length
         Straight
      Mini length
         Straight
         Full
      Long length
         Straight
         Full with deep slit

<u>Jacket Lengths:</u> Waist length
Long—just below rear
Long—finger tip
Peplum (with mini, straight skirts
 only)

<u>Styles of Jackets or
 Cardigans:</u> Button closed, snug fitting on hips
Wide lapels
Lapel of different color than rest of
 jacket
Deep "V" lapels

<u>Necklines:</u> Plunging
Fancy
"V" necks
Deep scoop
Backless
Open shirt collars

Sleeves:	Sleeveless
	Long pushed to three-quarter length
	Cut out
	Fancy

Colors

Core	Accent
Electric red	Electric blue
Black	Ice pink
White	Peach
Electric pink	Silver
Hot turquoise	Gold
Emerald green	Hot yellow
Purple	

Metallic colors are good colors for evening wear. Ice pink and peach are great soft sexy looks for a change of pace or to wear with black.

Prints

Bright abstract prints
Animal or jungle prints
Jacquard

Fabrics

Angora	Silks
Knits that hug	Lamé
Satin	Rayon
Jersey knit	Sequins
Raw silk	Wool crepe
Soft leather	Lycra blends

Crushable and/or body hugging fabrics.

Makeup

Try the basic makeup application (page 118) for a while. Notice the comments. The glamour option (page 121) is also excellent for your style.

Lip color: Fuchsia
               Red
               Any and all brights

Hair

Layered around the face
Jaw length or longer
Full and not too controlled
Can be styled over part of the face.
For examples see illustrations 40A, B and C.

Accessory Wardrobe

"Basic" refers to gold, silver and black.

Necklaces: 16-inch long, shaped collar at least 1 inch
thick
      1 Each basic
30-inch long large chain at least 1/2 inch
thick
      1 Each basic

Earrings: Quarter to silver dollar size
      1 Pair in each basic
Large hoops
      1 Pair in each basic
Shoulder dusters
      1 Pair in each basic

Bracelets: Large wide slip-ons or bands
      1 Each basic
      2 Accent colors with a basic

Pins: Larger than silver dollar
      1 Each basic

Belts: Soft leather, 2 inches wide
      1 Black
      1 Red
      1 In two accent colors
      1 Black with gold
      1 Black with silver

Shoes:	Pumps
	1 Pair black
	1 Pair textured light accent color
	1 Pair bright accent color
	High Heels
	1 Pair black
	Flats
	1 Pair black
	1 Pair textured light accent color
	1 Pair bright accent color

| Purses: | Two-tone black |
| | Two-tone light color |

Nylons:	Off black
	Charcoal
	Silver-gray
	Cream
	Suntan

This style can wear textured or suntan with a mini skirt for a sexy evening look.

<u>Detachable shoulder pads</u>

<u>Sleevebands</u>

When selecting the way you want to accessorize an outfit use the suggestions on page 107. The suggestions best for your style use one large finishing accessory (casual or evening) or three finishing accessories (office).

4

TIME TO TAKE ACTION

Get Rid Of The Old To Make Way For The New!

1. Clean out your closet making three piles of clothing.

Pile A. Clothes that look worn, don't fit or are in the wrong proportion.

Pile B. All the clothes that need mending or alterations. This includes all the clothes in good shape— the ones you like but need mending and all clothes that can be altered to the correct proportion.

Pile C. Keepers.

2. Put pile "A" in a box and get it out of your way. It may be that you are hesitant to take this box to a charity or a resale shop right away, but at least get it out of your sight.

3. Put pile "B" in a box and put it into the car. I strongly suggest that you take these to a dry cleaners or an alterations person and have them done. Waiting until you have time to do them will hinder all of the effort you are making. If you like to sew or have a friend or relative that does then get started in that direction. If you tend to let this type of chore wait, then go ahead and take the clothes to a professional. You will have wearable clothing for a lot less than if you spent money on a new outfit.

4. Hang pile "C" back in the closet. Separate by

blouses/tops, jackets, skirts, pants, dresses, putting all solids together and then all prints. All clothes should be on sturdy hangers (not wire ones) to keep them in good shape.

All of the pile "C" clothes should have the correct proportion. If jackets and skirts are not the correct proportions, put them with pile "A." If they can be corrected put them with pile "B."

Making New Looks From Existing Clothes

The first step in creating a new wardrobe is like putting a puzzle together. Begin by taking a favorite skirt and laying it on the bed with one of your favorite blouses. Don't worry about the colors or the fabrics, just put your two favorites together. On the "tie in" accessory sheet on page 250 write down those two colors as a team.

Let's say your favorite skirt is a classic length straight skirt from your jade suit (the jacket is the wrong length so you have discarded it). Your favorite blouse is a fuchsia silk with a notched neckline. You then write down the colors fuchsia and jade as a team. Now put your next favorite blouse with the jade skirt (let's say it's cream) and write those two colors down as a team. Once you have gone through all the tops, change to a different skirt and repeat the entire process. When you have no more skirts go through the process with your pants. You may well find that you have repeat teams. There is no need to write them down again if this is so. If pant outfits are less important to your wardrobe, then you don't need to do all of them; just do your favorites. You may ask a friend to do this with you.

Now you need to add your jackets to the teams. There is a space provided at the far right of the form. If you have more jackets than the space provides just select your four favorites for now and when the process is clear to you, go back and add the others to your list based on the example given. Your "tie-in" accessory sheet should look something like this.

Example Tie-In Accessories Worksheet

Bottoms	Tops	Jackets
Jade skirt	Fuchsia blouse	Black, cream, red, cobalt
Jade skirt	Cream blouse	Black, cream, red, cobalt
Black pant	Fuchsia blouse	Black, cream, red, cobalt
Black pant	Cream blouse	Black, cream, red, cobalt

Tie-In Accessories Worksheet

Bottoms	Tops	Jackets

Identify Your Accessory Needs

1. You need solid-colored belts to match your jackets. They don't have to match perfectly to work well. They also don't need to be expensive; sashes and cloth velcro belts work well. Based on the example Tie-In Worksheet you would need one black, one cream, one red, and one cobalt belt.

2. You need accessory sets to tie each team together (see page 107 for a reminder of ways to do this). The easiest, most popular and most valuable ways are to either select a neckpiece and bring one of the colors down in a belt or select a multi-colored belt and wear a basic earring.

Looking at your accessory Tie-In Worksheet you can tell what colors of accessory sets you need to create outfits. For example: The team of jade and fuchsia could be tied together with a pin in cobalt, jade, fuchsia and silver; a cobalt belt and a silver earring. Add the black jacket and change the belt to black, put on basic silver jewelry or a neckpiece with black, jade and fuchsia and you have a completely different outfit. If you wear the cream jacket with the jade skirt, fuchsia blouse combination, change to a cream belt and pearls. You can use any one of the ten ways to finish an outfit (see page 107). This is what women pay designers lots of money to do for them.

When you get to the jade, fuchsia and red combination, you may decide that this arrangement will not work. Believe it or not, some styles blend these colors successfully. I have a Dynamo client who combined a fuchsia jacket; red blouse; jade pants; black, red, fuchsia and jade scarf with a black belt and earrings. Even her most conservative of friends thought it was a new wonderful outfit. In truth, all the pieces but the scarf came from her closet and had been worn many times before. I am not saying that you will love this color combination. I am saying not to limit your color combinations until you give them a try.

All colors do go together; it is only your style that decides if it is right for you. Be sure you eliminate items only after you have seen these colors put together with good accessories. One of the best ways to do this is to call a local boutique or department store, tell them you want to bring some clothes in to accessorize. If they don't welcome the chance to help you, go to a different store.

Be sure you walk in knowing the color teams you want to put together and bring a few that you are unsure about also. Remember the lady who helps you has different taste than you do. In addition, she probably has less knowledge than you now have of how to put the outfits together. I would suggest taking your book with you. This is fun and you learn while you teach. You may be able to buy three sets of accessories which give you more than a dozen outfits.

3. A few shortcuts to tie new clothes in with your wardrobe:

•When you buy a print skirt or pant, buy a neckpiece in one of the colors in the skirt.

•When you buy a solid pant or skirt, buy a neckpiece in the same color.

•When you buy a solid color dress, buy a neckpiece with the dress color and a jacket color you have at home.

•When you buy a blouse, buy a multi-colored belt that has your blouse color in it.

Basic Wardrobe All Styles

As you developed your tie-ins you may have noticed that you were lacking some important basic clothes. Most often it's jackets that women are without because all the jackets owned were in the wrong length. A good basic wardrobe has these foundation pieces:
 • The basic accessories for your style.
 • 1 Long jacket
 • 1 Core colored blouse (white or cream is best).
 • 2 Accent blouses.
 • 1 Classic length solid-colored skirt (to match jacket if you want a suit).
 • 1 Printed or textured classic or long length skirt (ideally with the color of your jacket in it).
 • 1 Pair core color slacks.
 • 1 Other solid skirt in classic or long length.
 • 1 Belt that closely matches jacket.
 • 1 Solid-colored neckpiece in one of the colors found in the print skirt.

After you have these basics, additional pieces should be added in the same sequence. First a second jacket, then a second core colored blouse, etc.

For A More Casual Wardrobe

Replace the basic wardrobe jacket with a cardigan and the skirts with pants or mini-skirts. With these eight pieces of clothing and the accessories you could easily create 30 completely different-looking and wonderful outfits. I have done as many as 121 outfits by simply increasing the accessory wardrobe.

Each time you purchase a new garment, buy tie-in

accessories to work with your existing clothes. Because you know your proportions are right, you don't have to have your clothes with you.

When you do decide to add a jacket, dress, skirt etc. you will be building from a strong beginning and mistakes just won't happen. The addition of one piece to such a foundation creates many outfits instead of just one.

Take a breath. You have learned a lot. Now it is time to act on your learning. If you need to start with only one accessory set, that's okay. Just take the first step. Get rid of the old to make way for the new. No excuses, you can do it. Confidence will grow along the way—so will your beauty.

Why Women Settle For Looking Less Than Their Best

The three most common excuses women give for settling for less are: Time, money and weight.

Throughout the life of your children you hope you will be there for the "good" and "bad" times. Life rarely works out that way, but there is a life long gift you can give your children that will help them through anything, whether you can be with them or not. This gift will help them overcome heartache and disappointment and come out on top. It will help them to see the good in others and find happiness no matter what life throws their way. If you give your children the gift of self esteem you are indeed a terrific parent. No gift of time or money is more precious.

Did you know that ninety percent of your child's learning up until the age of 12 is through role modeling? If you set the example that you are not happy with yourself, you teach your children to be unhappy with themselves. If you put yourself down, they learn to put themselves down.

If you don't take care of yourself and the way you look, they learn that it is unimportant. So when mothers say they don't have time to work out or do their hair or get their nails done, my response is that you are being more selfish by not taking care of yourself. You are hindering your children's opportunity to grow up with a positive self esteem as well as depriving them of a happier home with a happier, healthier and more rested mom.

If time is your reason but you aren't a mother. simply know that you will have less happy and successful relationships if you don't take time to be your best.

The "money" reason for not taking action to improve your life is common. It is tough getting rid of a jacket you bought last season because it's the wrong length. I suggest you put it into the back of the closet, then compare it later to your perfected wardrobe. You'll be surprised how you feel about it then. I know single mothers raising three kids on low pay who have found the money— because it was important to them. I know middle class business women, single and earning a good salary, who have not been able to find the money. We can't all do it as quickly as we may wish, but if you find it important enough you will find the money to do it. Make taking action a priority for yourself. If I haven't emphasized it enough let me tell you again that you are worth it and that it will create wonders in your life.

Carrying extra weight is a consistent complaint of women. Too many times we want to shed pounds before buying nice clothes. Weight control counselors all agree that self acceptance is essential to losing and keeping off pounds. If you were to buy nice clothes now, even if you are 50 pounds overweight, you would look better and feel better. You would be more motivated to take care of yourself, exercise and eat right. If you have to alter your clothes as you go down in size, so what? You would have to buy new clothes anyway when you got to your desired weight. I had a client four years ago who was a size 14 and said, "I'll be a size 8 by next year." She purchased a beautiful and compact wardrobe in size 14. After 10 months and three alterations she still had the quality clothes. Money is not the issue here, it's self esteem. If you really want to lose the weight, take time to look good now. Why paddle up stream when you don't have to?

5

ENVIRONMENT

This section of the book examines how you live, where you live, and the roles you play in life. A teacher of second graders in South Dakota does not have the same wardrobe needs as a public relations director in New York—even if they have the same style. On the other hand, two second grade teachers in Mississippi with different styles don't have the same wardrobe needs either. An executive with a newborn baby has different needs than one with grown children. Sometimes you need to compromise your style to fit your environment. The degree of compromise is up to you.

Compromise is often needed for you to be seen as a winner, a team player, someone who has something to offer the company, organization or relationship. As a result of your compromise, others will gain or increase respect for your knowledge, professionalism, confidence, trustworthiness and your word. If you do make the decision to adjust your style to better fit your environment it shows that you are seeing yourself through the eyes of the world around you. This replaces guesswork with educated decisions.

At work or in your personal life you live with the expectations of others. Understanding what is expected of you is necessary for whatever success you seek. When you decide to dress ignoring the expectations of your environment, you are communicating that you are an individual of unique qualities. You are also communicating that you are rebellious, not a team player and not concerned about what others want or think. Then again, if you were to continue to dress in the same style and put yourself into a different environment you may well be perceived in exactly the opposite light.

One woman's success story resulted from the choice to ignore environment and to dress one hundred percent for her style. When I met Amy she was an advertising sales representative for a local magazine. After discovering her style to be #6 (The Individualist), I showed her ideal examples of her style. She loved the clothes and felt wonderful in them. Being artistic, off-beat and a non-conformist, we talked about the negatives of dressing this way in her job and that it would probably hurt her career in advertising. We then discussed compromise. She made the decision not to compromise. She believed in herself and believed that it would work out. She felt great in the artistic type clothes. Feeling good meant to her that she would do well.

Her sales did not decline, but she found that different people were attracted to her, that she was losing interest in advertising and that her relationship with her husband was becoming more like it was when they first met. Three months later Amy was working as a display specialist for an art gallery. Five years later Amy is now the manager for the art institute in her town, has a three year old daughter, a joyful marriage and more money with less stress. By being herself she attracted people looking for her natural talents. She began doing work that she loved and success followed.

Amy was brave, she made the decision to "buck" the system knowing that she might lose respect in her work. She made the decision consciously. I don't recommend it for everyone but it may be worth considering if you discover that your environment is in direct conflict with your style.

Then there is the choice to *completely ignore* your own style which can be a dangerous thing to do to your self esteem, but there may be occasions in which it can be of use to get you what you want. If you deny yourself for a long period of time it communicates that you are fearful, lacking confidence, a follower, unreliable, and self-involved.

Trish decided to ignore her style successfully when she interviewed for a position as a sales representative of office machines. She had been a successful secretary for ten years and was tired of the pay and the hours. Trish was confident that she would do a bang-up job as a salesperson. The company specifically advertised for self-starting, reliable, organized and ambitious applicants. Although she felt she was all of these things she had no experience in sales. Trish is the Gentlewoman style. Having learned the advantages of projecting her own style she was not willing to give it up even if she did get the job. In fact, Trish believed it was what would make her successful at sales. She decided to dress in a combination of the Straight Shooter and the Achiever to communicate more reliability, organization, and ambition.

After three interviews Trish was offered the job. The genius of her plan was that she dressed completely as the Gentlewoman when she went in to discuss salary and benefits. Although Trish had no prior experience, she ended up with the highest starting package the company had offered to date. In three years she was promoted to regional manager and now works as national sales manager for the competition.

Trish felt that by giving the interviewers what they

wanted she was opening the door to getting what she wanted. This does not apply to every situation. You will have to decide for yourself. Isn't it nice to know that your destiny is more in your hands now than ever before—even if it is scary!

Work Environment

When you enter the working world you are not given an instruction booklet, but every employer assumes certain things. The problem is those "things" are rarely if ever communicated to you. It is not uncommon for a person to work for 15 to 20 years for the same company and then discover that she was passed up for opportunities because what the boss wanted and what she thought the boss wanted were two different things. The best way to avoid this miscommunication and to feel appreciated for the work you do is to educate yourself on what to expect.

There are thousands of different jobs. Yet your career will fall into one or more of the following "worlds": **Corporate, Communicative, Creative.** There are different unwritten rules and expectations for each of these. The expectations of your world may fit your style very well, in which case you will have little to adjust in your style. If there is a conflict between your style and your environment you have some things to consider.

Whether you dress one hundred percent for your style, one hundred percent for your world or a combination, your decision can be a positive, wonderful experience. No one is better than the other. If you make your choice on the basis of what you truly want for yourself, you will be taking charge of your life. It is a brave and winning thing to do.

CORPORATE

Don't get hung up on the label I have given this work area. Corporate world in this case refers to anyone who is involved with trade or services. People in this environment admire ambition, organization, confidence, and conscientiousness. It also is a world that promotes people who are supporters of tradition, have above average skills and know how to direct others.

The ideal styles for the corporate environment are:

The Achiever. It is vital for this style to recognize the importance of communication to success. Working on approachability, appreciation and consideration will be of major benefit.

The Straight Shooter. If this style wants to advance or be appreciated, then taking time for herself and making her appearance a priority will increase her chances drastically.

Those who will most benefit from adjusting their style for the corporate world are:

The Individualist. Her individualism will be a threat in this world and she will be seen as unreliable.

The Innocent. This style will often be put on the defensive and will have to turn into a fighter in order to survive.

The Knockout. Sensuality is a threat to all women in this world. It also is a deterrent to respect from men.

COMMUNICATIVE

If you are in an environment that requires you to talk or listen to others you have communication requirements in your field. In today's work force this includes practically all of us. Success in this world requires you to appear honest, caring, understanding, enthusiastic, flexible, open minded, and practical. You will shine in a communications world if you are a team player, service-oriented, a doer, a supporter, a people person and have good listening skills.

The ideal styles for this environment are:

<u>The Gentlewoman.</u> This style will need to work on developing some toughness. Setting the precedent that she is always available with a shoulder to cry on can get her into too many fixes at work. Learn the value of saying "No."

<u>The All American.</u> This style needs to work on calming herself when talking with others. Her spirit will be respected by superiors if she avoids being too much of a cheerleader.

Those who will most benefit from adjusting their style for the communication world are:

<u>The Individualist.</u> This style too often is seen as a rebel and therefore can be shut out of the team or group effort to succeed. Many people feel they can't relate to the Individualist.

<u>The Knockout.</u> The expression of super confidence as a woman creates a feeling of unapproachability. It is interpreted as not needing help from anyone. Modifying dress and playing down sexiness at work will permit this style to be included as part of the team.

CREATIVE

Any job that asks you to be original is in the

creative world. This can simply mean that you are asked to come up with an original idea or a new solution to a problem, or it can mean creating something from nothing. To be a success in this environment is to express individuality, originality, problem-solving ability, intuitiveness, ability to work alone and unguided and to have the strength of your beliefs.

Being a lover of the arts, I hate to admit it, but our society does not support the attitudes of the artistic. The fact that artists are nonconformists, rebellious, activists, and are not time-conscious or money-hungry is discomforting for most people. Don't take this as a put-down. I mention it simply to remind you that people of your style have to be even braver and more of a trail-blazing nature in order to succeed. Either that or you find a level of conformity in which you are comfortable.

The ideal styles for this environment are:

The Individualist. No matter how much genius there is in your talent to make money you must adapt to the corporate and communicative mainstream. After you are financially successful—if that is what you want—you can hire someone to do your business and deal with people. Many talented artists have been forced to put their creative passion on hold in order to meet their family responsibilities. You can prevent this by spending some time in the corporate or communication world and then bring that knowledge into your creative undertakings.

The Dynamo. You will shine in a creative world that has glamour, entertainment, or pizzazz. If you get to the point in your life where you have a hard time giving up the limelight to others, or feel you have something others just don't have, you will be creating a more difficult path for yourself. Learning the advantages of the corporate world will help you.

The Knockout. You could really enjoy this world because creative people are more accepting of the differences in people. Sexy women are a threat to many women in America. The entertainment industry has labeled sexy women "shallow" or "the other woman." The open-mindedness of the creative world could be a great place for you if you keep yourself open to learning.

Those who will most benefit from adjusting their style for the creative world are:

The Straight Shooter. Your practicality, ideals and standards can be seen as inflexible in a world where flexibility is held in high regard.

The Innocent. Innocence is not a respected or sought after trait in this world and is usually seen as lack of awareness and concern.

The Elegant Lady. Changing this style for the creative world will depend on whether or not you wish to be seen as creative or prefer to organize and lead. The former needs a style change to be appropriate; the latter does not.

WHICH WORLD IS YOUR WORLD?

As you probably have already noticed, these three environments are intertwined. Most corporate worlds require a high level of communication. Most communication worlds either deal with corporate or creative people on a daily basis. Creative worlds exist within a corporate/communicative structure. Which of these three worlds best describes the world you work in at this time?

1._____

2._____

3._____

Which of these worlds would you most enjoy working in?

1._____

2._____

3._____

If you would like your style to work better for you on the job, adopt a couple of the elements from one of the ideal styles for the environment you are in.

Don't diminish the importance of communication if you are in finance, accounting, banking or what you may consider a truly corporate world.

Don't diminish the importance of professionalism if you are a teacher, social worker or entrepreneur and consider your world only one of communication.

If you are a hairdresser, interior designer, architect, or fashion designer, communication skills will bring you more business than your talent alone.

If you would like your style to work better for you on the job, adopt a couple of the elements from one of the ideal styles for the environment you are in.

The Most Common And Most Costly Image Mistakes At Work

Mistake: Dressing too severely or in a masculine fashion—communicating that you aren't approachable. (In all three worlds.)

To improve: Open up collars and push sleeves to three-quarter length. When wearing a black suit or blazer, either wear a scarf or a soft pastel (or blue colored) blouse, with pearls. Put a few long printed skirts in your wardrobe to be worn with your jackets. Try two-piece dresses with a jacket over the top. Stay away from pants suits.

Mistake: Dressing in pants of any type—communicating that you are a subordinate, lack ambition, unprofessional.

To improve: Don't wear pants. If you must, at least cover your butt (figuratively and literally) with a jacket or cardigan. Wear a long skirt length with flat shoes and a long jacket if comfort is your principal concern.

Mistake: Wearing worn clothes—communicating a lack of confidence, intelligence, and success at what you do. (In all three worlds.)

To Improve: Give worn clothes away, even if it means you have to wear the same outfit(s) until you can replace them. Wearing the same garment in good shape is infinitely better than wearing a variety of worn clothes. People do notice balled fabric, loose hems and seams that are worn .

Mistake: Being too high fashion—communicating that it is more important to be attractive than professional, intelligent or respected.

To improve: Wear the long length of jacket. Adopt the classic length of skirt. Don't adjust colors to what is "In."

Mistake: Dressing in too sexy a fashion, such as body-hugging clothes, skirts that are too short, heels above 2 1/2 inches or necklines that go below the breast bone (which the show L.A. Law brought back in to fashion). Dressing in this fashion communicates that you want to be seen and treated by men as an alluring woman more than as a professional, intelligent woman deserving respect. (Especially in the Corporate and Communication worlds.)

To improve: Adopt the mid-knee classic skirt length. Use the fit guidelines given under proportion for skirts, blouses, necklines etc. Keep the heels at two inches or less during business hours.

Mistake: Dressing like you did in college or in too young a fashion—communicating a lack of knowledge, savvy, business sense, reliability, work ethic and original thought.

To improve: Wear jackets. Pull your hair back or wear it above the shoulder. Don't wear mini-skirts or shorts. Buy some qulaity pieces as soon as possible.

Mistake: Wearing more than one piece of very bold or noisy jewelry—communicating a demand for attention and recognition for your flair (which may be fine in the creative world).

To improve: If you love bold jewelry keep it quiet or down to one major piece.

Mistake: Not finishing an outfit—communicating lack of organization, professionalism, calmness, and success. (In all three worlds.)

To improve: Make buying of your basic accessories a priority. Use one of the ten different ways for accessorizing any outfit.

Mistake: Not wearing a jacket with your outfits—communicating lack of ambition, naivete in business, lack of leadership, lack of professionalism, and lack of organization. There are casual times at work when a jacket is not needed with a dress or skirt. You need to identify the times you want to look more professional.

To improve: Get two jackets into your wardrobe. Go for the long length and solid colors.

Mistake: Wearing skin tone nylons—communicating disorganization, an unfinished look, and a desire to show off the legs.

To improve: Wear hose the same tone as your hemline (see page 96).

Mistake: Smoking—communicating disregard for your health. With today's emphasis on healthy indoor environments, the person who smokes in the presence of nonsmokers shows a lack of consideration.

To improve: Make an extra effort not to smoke in front of co-workers and remember to keep your clothes and breath as free of smoke odors as possible.

Mistake: Other common mistakes often overlooked are bad breath, body odors, undesirable eating habits, strong perfume, gum chewing, coughing, too much makeup—communicating that you are thoughtless about the opinions of others even though the fault may be an oversight on your part.

To improve: Take steps to prevent annoying other people with habits that you can correct. Take the time to consider your appearance and clothes.

Personal Environment

It is desirable that your personal environment be a place where you can be yourself in comfort. While kicking off your shoes is relaxing, some women forget the importance of nonverbal communication in the home and concern themselves with it only at work.

Which do you take the most time to look good for, your job or your husband? Do you ever go without doing your hair, taking a shower or washing your face when you take your kids to soccer practice? Would you do that at work?

Remember when you first fell in love with your partner? Did you let him see you at your worst often if at all? Were you in better shape? Did you touch him more? Did you listen more? Unfortunately, too many women let themselves "go" and then wonder why they aren't as happy as when they first fell in love. In addition, while courting many women present themselves in a manner they think men will like rather than how they prefer to be themselves.

While it is important to please the people you love, their recommendations as to what you should wear should not govern your decisions. The people who truly love you will be most pleased if you develop the confidence to be yourself. That means just because your mother has a great sense of style, it does not mean that you should adopt hers as your own. People who are close are usually most supportive if you include them in your learning because they feel they have contributed to your progress.

Many women dress for their spouses, but if you don't feel comfortable dressing that way, it will benefit your self esteem to at least partially assert your own style. A lot of men have fantasies as to how they want their women to look. The two big ones are long hair and sexy or snug-fitting clothes.

Some men on the other hand have great classic taste and if you just direct them with your elements of style they will be able to buy you some wonderful pieces. I have had many clients whose spouses refused years ago to ever buy them clothes again. But after discovering their style and giving their husbands specific guidelines the women have been delighted with the gifts they've received, and the men have felt pleased with the acknowledgments that their choices were suitable.

If you are single, all I can say is that if you want to attract someone to love you for who you are—be yourself in your nonverbal communication and dress.

My suggestions for successful dressing in your personal life are:

1. When you become a mother, you may want to adapt to a more casual style than your core style offers. You can do this by moving to the fabrics of your style that are washable. Another option is to use two elements of the Straight Shooter or the All American, one of which should be fabric.

2. Dress in your style as much as you can.

3. Be open to dressing for your partner except at work.

4. Provide those who love you with as many measurements and guidelines as you can. Be sure you give them the lengths, styles, and colors you need.

5. Let people know that you are trying to improve your self image and ask for their support.

6. Ask loved ones not to buy work clothes for you, unless you have the type of relationship in which they welcome guidance.

7. Take the way you look, even in sweats, more to heart. Do it for your children, your lover, your loved ones, and yourself in order to gain more respect, consideration and appreciation from each.

8. Playing with different looks and different styles to fit your moods can also be fun and puts a little spice in your life.

6

HOW TO CROSS OVER FROM ONE STYLE TO ANOTHER

The following nine illustrations are examples of how to cross over from one style to another by "adopting" elements. At least two elements need to be adopted to be successful.

In each case I have retained one item of clothing from the original model in order to demonstrate the money that can be saved in the cross over process.

You can compare the cross-over with the original by turning to the page showing the original model. (It is indicated on each cross over.)

When you choose to adopt elements of another style you should realize that you are taking on the characteristics as well. (At least you are projecting them.) Therefore it is worthwhile to read what the traits are for the style you are adopting.

Straight Shooter → Gentlewoman

Elements adopted:
Print
Proportion (sleeves,
neckline)
Accessories
Fabric

<u>Jacket:</u> Navy blue wool flannel with silver buttons.
<u>Skirt:</u> Navy, dusty rose, burgundy, cream, rayon, Victorian print.
<u>Shell:</u> Dusty rose angora.
<u>Pocket square:</u> Cream lace.
<u>Brooch:</u> Gold with pearl drop.
<u>Earrings:</u> Pear Drops.
<u>Hose:</u> Charcoal
<u>Shoes:</u> Navy pumps.

Creating a softer more feminine look.

Original model to compare with is illustration 32C on page 145.

Illustration #41

All American → Individualist

Elements adopted:
Color
Fabric
Hair
Accessories

Jacket: Navy raw silk.
Skirt: Dark olive leather.
Cowl neck: Coral.
Scarf: Olive, navy, dark brown and coral.
Belt: Dark brown.
Earrings: Copper.
Bracelet: Copper.
Hose: Charcoal.
Shoes: Two tone, olive and brown.

Creating a funkier more artistic look.

Original model to compare with is illustration 33B on page 157.

Illustration #42

Achiever ➜ Dynamo

Elements adopted:
  Color
  Fabric
  Hair
  Accessories

<u>Skirt:</u> Charcoal worsted wool.
<u>Sweater:</u> White with magenta, cornflower blue, charcoal and black suede leaves.
<u>Earrings:</u> Magenta suede leaves.
<u>Bracelet:</u> Magenta
<u>Hose:</u> Charcoal
<u>Shoes:</u> Black

Creating a more dramatic eye-catching look.

Original model to compare with is illustration 34B on page 168.

Illustration #43

Elegant Lady → All American

Elements adopted:
   Print
   Color

<u>Sweater:</u> Cream, cotton, wool blend, cowl neck.
<u>Skirt:</u> Cream, marino wool.
<u>Cardigan:</u> Cream with cobalt stripe at shoulder, all other stripes are orange, cotton blend.
<u>Earrings:</u> Cobalt.
<u>Belt:</u> Cobalt
<u>Hose:</u> Cream
<u>Shoes:</u> Cream

Creating a more spunky and fresh look.

Original model to compare with is illustration 35B on page 179.

Illustration #44

Dynamo → Straight Shooter

Elements Adopted:
Color
Fabric
Hair

<u>Dress:</u> Emerald jersey.
<u>Cardigan:</u> Navy cotton knit.
<u>Pins:</u> Silver, nine small ones bunched together.
<u>Belt:</u> Navy and emerald knit wrap.
<u>Earring:</u> Silver and navy.
<u>Headband:</u> Navy.
<u>Hose:</u> Charcoal.
<u>Shoes:</u> Navy.

Creating a more casual, practical look.

Original model to compare with is illustration 36A on page 191.

Illustration #45

Individualist → Innocent

Elements adopted:
   Color
   Print
   Hair
   Accessories

<u>Sweater:</u> Soft pink with ivory collar, rayon.
<u>Skirt:</u> Medium brown, heavy cotton.
<u>Jacket:</u> Soft pink, ivory, and brown challis.
<u>Necklace:</u> Gold.
<u>Earrings:</u> Gold and rose.
<u>Belt:</u> Ivory
<u>Bracelet:</u> Pearl
<u>Nylons:</u> Silver gray.
<u>Shoes:</u> Brown.

Creating a younger, sweet look.

Original model to compare with is illustration 37B on page 205.

Illustration #46

Gentlewoman ➜ Knockout

Elements adopted:
  Proportion (hem and
    neckline).
  Accessories
  Hair

Skirt: Mallard, burgundy,
soft pink on pearl gray
background, chiffon.
Blouse: Soft gray satin.
Earrings: Silver and
burgundy.
Hose: Gray.
Shoes: Gray.

Creating a more
alluring, sexy look.

Original model to
compare with is
iIllustration 38C on page
216.

Illustration #47

Innocent → Achiever

Elements adopted:
   Proportion (jacket
      and neckline).
   Color
   Fabrics
   Makeup (soft red
      lipstick).

Skirt: Gray rayon crepe.
Blouse: Teal blue.
Jacket: Light true red,
soft wool flannel.
Belt: Light true red.
Necklace: Silver beads.
Earrings: Silver.
Hose: Gray.
Shoes: Gray.

Creating a more organized, professional look.

Original model to compare with is illustration 39C on page 228.

Illustration #48

Knockout → Elegant Lady

Elements adopted:
    Color.
    Proportion (hem and
        neckline).
    Accessories.
    Hair.

Blouse: Ivory silk.
Skirt: Gray, light weight flannel.
Jacket: Electric pink, wool crepe.
Earrings: Pearl and pewter.
Pin: Pearl and pewter.
Watch: Pewter bracelet.
Hose: Ivory.
Shoes: Ivory.

Creating a more gracious, classy look.

Original model to compare with is illustration 40B on page 240.

Illustration #49

CONCLUSION

If you believe you're beautiful, you are. It really is all in your state of mind. I hope you have found ways to express your inner beauty and wonder while reading this book. I hope that you have made your life easier, gotten rid of some misconceptions and had fun along the way. My desire has been to impart knowledge and skills so that you can be in control of how others see you, and that your appearance is now a conscious choice instead of haphazard guessing.

I wish I were with you to see the results of your travels through these pages, to hear the stories of frustration, growth, amazement and comprehension. I would love to stand some of you in front of the mirror and show you all your points of beauty until you believed them. Every time I heard a negative remark, I would roll my eyes and convince you how silly you were and how much you have to offer by being you.

No matter what style you are I know I would like to meet you because if you bought this book you are seeking change and growth. With all our differences that is an admirable trait in everyone. I applaud your courage to seek change. I hope you have found the incentive to make that change.

If you have a story to tell me, I hope you drop me a line; I would love to hear it.

Training • Speaking • Consulting

Thousands of people have been inspired and empowered by attending seminars with Teri Twitty-Villani. Teri is praised for her enthusiasm and practicality.
Subjects include:

Shut Up And Let Them Buy
• Listening your way to sales success.

Teams Work
• Increase employee productivity and quality.

Communication: The Conflict Prevention Medicine
• The art all winners have in common.

And of course:

Appearances Speak Louder Than Words
• A common sense approach to developing a
  winning image.

If you would like further information for your company or organization please write to:

Voyager Press
829 N. W. 19th
Portland, Oregon 97209
Or call: (503) 274-2880